GRADE

3

ISTEP+ Finish Line

English/Language Arts

 Continental Press

Credits

Illustrations: Page 25: Estella Hickman; Page 44, 140: Michael Fink; Page 71, 77, 92: Rob Williams; Page 74, 104, 118, 123, 128, 133, 137, 157, 164, 173: Laurie Conley; Page 89, 143, 145: Harry Norcross: Page 97, 161: Murray Callahan; Page 114: James McConnell; Page 195: Ruth Flanigan; Page 221: U.S. Fish and Wildlife Service; Page 235: Sally Springer.

Photos: Cover, title page: *Michigan City Lighthouse, Michigan City, IN,* www.stockexpert.com/soupstock; Page 23: www.istockphoto.com/clinch; Page 31: www.photos.com; Page 48 *tiger:* www.shutterstock.com, Tiago Jorge da Silva Estima; *map:* www.istockphoto.com/emptyclouds; Page 49: www.shutterstock.com, nialat; Page 53 *left:* www.shutterstock.com, Dennis Donohue; *right:* www.shutterstock.com, Gary Potts; Page 54: www.istock.com/tacojim; Page 55 *map:* Courtesy of National Park Service; Page 61: www.shutterstock.com, Cindy Hughes; Page 65: Associated Press; Page 67: Royalty-Free/Corbis; Page 75: www.istockphoto.com/945ontwerp; Page 80: Zach Delph; Page 83: www.istockphoto.com/compassandcamera; Page 85: www.shutterstock.com, Donald R. Swartz; Page 87: www.shutterstock.com, Tom C. Amon; Page 98: www.shutterstock.com, Goran Kapor; Page 101: www.shutterstock.com, John Kirinic; Page 105: www.shutterstock.com, signorina; Page 148: www.photos.com; Page 167: www.shutterstock.com, Dhoxax; Page 190: Getty Images; Page 232: www.istockphoto.com/GlennHarris; Page 234: www.istockhoto.com/jeryltan.

ISBN 978-0-8454-6107-5

Contents

Welcome to ISTEP+ Finish Line English/Language Arts!

Everyone wants to do well on tests. Tests help your teacher and school see the progress you are making. They also help you get ready for the next step in school. This book will help you get ready for the *ISTEP+ English/Language Arts Test.* On the test, you will read passages and answer multiple-choice questions about them. And you will write answers, called *short responses*.

The lessons in this book will help you improve your skills in vocabulary, reading, and writing. The lessons are in three parts.

- The first part of the lesson introduces the reading or writing skill you are going to study and explains what it is and how you use it.

- The second part is called Guided Practice. You will get more than just practice here; you will get help. You will read a story, poem, or nonfiction article and answer questions about it. After each question, the correct answer will be explained to you. So you will answer questions and find out right away if you are right. You also will learn why one answer is right and others are not.

- The third part is called Test Yourself. This time you will read a passage and answer the questions on your own. First, you will answer several multiple-choice questions, and then you will write an answer to a question.

Once you have completed the lessons, you'll take a practice test to see what you have learned.

Now you are ready to begin. Good luck!

Unit 1
Understanding Words

This unit will help you answer vocabulary questions on tests. You already have a big vocabulary that you use when you talk, listen, read, and write. On a test, you will be asked which words or parts of words have the same sound. Other questions will ask what a word or phrase means. If you know the word or phrase, it will be easy to answer the question. But if you're not sure of the meaning, you need another way to find the answer.

1 **Phonics**   This lesson tells you about the way sounds and letters go together to make words. In the English language, letters can stand for different sounds in different words. When you take a test, say the words to yourself and listen to the sounds before you mark your answer choice. You will also learn more about word families and words with several syllables.

2 **Word Parts**   This lesson tells you about ways to form words using prefixes, suffixes, root words, compound words, and contractions. You can use what you know about these topics to figure out the meaning of a word on a test.

3 **Words in Context**   This lesson shows you how to use information in the things you read to figure out the meaning of a word you don't know. You will learn about word clues in the form of synonyms and antonyms. You'll also learn about multiple-meaning words and homophones.

4 **Rules of English**   This lesson tells you about rules of English such as parts of speech, capital letters, subjects and predicates, and end marks and commas. Knowing these rules gives you more control over what you read and write, and helps prepare you for questions you'll see on tests.

Phonics

Standards 3.1.1–3

Consonants

Consonant letters usually stand for one sound. The letters **c** and **g** can stand for two different sounds.

b	band		**n**	name
c	can		**p**	pan
c	cent	*c sounds like **s** before **e**, **i**, and **y***	**q**	quick
d	dog		**r**	ring
f	fan		**s**	sing
g	give		**t**	tank
g	gentle	*g sounds like **j** before **e**, **i**, and **y***	**v**	van
h	hand		**w**	wind
j	juice		**x**	box
k	kick		**y**	year
l	land		**z**	zoo
m	man			

Consonant digraphs are two letters that stand for one sound.

ch	chop	**ph**	phone	**th**	them
sh	ship	**th**	think	**gh**	laugh

Consonant blends are two letters that stand for two sounds. Usually the second letter and sound is **l** or **r**.

Blends with **l**	black, clay, flag, glad, play, slip
Blends with **r**	brick, crawl, dream, fry, great, prize, train

Some consonant letters are "silent." You don't hear them when you say the word.

write, **gh**ost, **k**not, **sc**ene, li**gh**t

Guided Practice

Say each word to yourself. The underlined part of the first word stands for a sound. Circle the letter for the word that has the same sound.

ca̲lendar

    A ice

    B chalk

    C certain

    D vacation

> Look for the letters after **c.** In *calendar,* **c** is followed by **a.** That means it is a hard **c** sound, like **k.** Say choice D to yourself. In *vacation,* **c** has a hard **c** sound. The correct choice is D.

tou̲g̲h̲

    A life

    B great

    C right

    D hanger

> Remember to think about the sounds, not the letters. Say *tough* to yourself. The sound at the end is like **f.** Choice C has the letters **gh.** But *right* does not have the sound **f.** The correct choice is A.

<u>wrap</u>

A wall

B rang

C white

D towel

In the word *wrap,* there is a "silent" letter, **w.** That means the word sounds the same as *rap.* Look for another word with the sound of **r.** The correct choice is B.

Vowels

Vowel letters stand for more than one sound. They are called <u>short</u> sounds and <u>long</u> sounds.

You hear short vowel sounds when there is a consonant sound after the vowel.

You hear long vowel sounds when there is a silent **e** after the consonant sound.

Short	Long
cap	cape
pen	Pete
bit	bite
not	note
cut	cute

The letter **y** can be a vowel sound, too. It can sound like long **e** or long **i.**

carry	try

Vowel **digraphs** are two vowels together that stand for one sound. Usually the sound is the long vowel sound of the first letter.

ai	paid	**ea**	meal	**ie**	die	**oe**	toe
ay	pay	**ee**	meet	**oa**	boat		

Vowel **diphthongs** are two vowel letters together that stand for a different sound. The same two letters can stand for different sounds. Look at **oo, ou** and **ow** in the chart.

au	cause	**oi**	coin	**ou**	loud
aw	paw	**oy**	boy	**ou**	soup
ei	eight	**oo**	book	**ow**	cow
ew	knew	**oo**	boot	**ow**	crow

Guided Practice

Say each word to yourself. The underlined part of the first word stands for a sound. Circle the letter for the word that has the same sound.

br<u>ai</u>n

  A clan

  B broil

  C cane

  D coat

Listen for the long **a** sound in *brain*. It is spelled with the digraph <u>ai</u>. The word *cane* has the long **a** sound, too. The correct choice is C.

crowd

    A proud

    B throw

    C throat

    D throne

There are two ways to say the diphthong ow. The word *crowd* has the same sound as *proud.* In fact, the words rhyme. That's a good way to tell that the vowel sounds are the same. The correct choice is A.

tie

    A boil

    B limp

    C sorry

    D slide

The digraph **ie** has the same long **i** sound as the word *slide.* So, choice D is the correct answer.

Word Families

Word families are words with common letters, sounds, or patterns. For example, the word *bell* and *yell* have the ending *-ell* in common. These words also rhyme. Recognizing word families helps you when pronouncing an unfamiliar word.

Guided Practice

Answer the following questions.

Read the sentence below.

> *The bell rang and the children began to yell as they ran to tell their teacher who won the race.*

Which word family do *bell, yell,* and *tell* belong to?

   A -en

   B -ing

   C -an

   D -ell

The word *children* belongs to the -en word family. The word *rang* belongs to the -an word family. No words in the sentence belong to the -ing word family. Choices A, B, C are incorrect. *Bell, yell,* and *tell* belong to the -ell word family. Choice D is correct.

Read the sentence below.

> *The light from the flashlight was bright in the dark night.*

Which word family do *light, bright,* and *night* belong to?

   A -ash

   B -in

   C -ar

   D -ight

Light, flashlight, and *bright* end in *-ight* and they rhyme. These words belong to the *-ight* word family. The correct choice is D.

Syllables

A *syllable* is a word part that creates a sound. Words can be made up of one syllable or many more. Knowing how to break a word into syllables helps you to say the word.

The word *light* creates one sound. It has one syllable. The word *tiger* creates two sounds. The first is *ti* and the second is *ger.* This word has two syllables.

Guided Practice

Read the passage below. Then answer the following questions.

Sam huddled under the bedcovers with his flashlight to finish reading his favorite book about knights. He had read the story so many times he could almost say it from memory.

Which of these words from the story has three syllables?

A Sam

B put

C under

D favorite

Sam and *put* create only one sound. These words have one syllable. Choices A and B are incorrect. The word *under* has two sounds. It has two syllables: un•der. Choice C is incorrect. The word *favorite* creates three sounds. It has three syllables: fav•o•rite. Choice D is correct.

Which of these words from the story has three syllables?

A bedcovers

B knight

C down

D could

The words *knight, down,* and *could* have one syllable. Choices B, C, and D are incorrect. The word *bedcovers* has three syllables: bed•cov•ers. The correct choice is A.

Test Yourself

Say each word to yourself. The underlined part of the first word stands for a sound. Circle the letter for the word that has the same sound.

1 dan<u>g</u>er

   A ghost

   B grand

   C dangle

   D general

2 sc<u>oo</u>p

   A look

   B song

   C group

   D ground

3 k<u>n</u>ock

A park

B locker

C kettle

D natural

4 gra<u>ph</u>

A careful

B rapid

C happen

D practice

5 thr<u>oa</u>t

A coil

B corn

C stone

D threat

6 <u>g</u>row

A glad

B agree

C angel

D garden

7 <u>c</u>ause

A awful

B castle

C chase

D amount

8 p<u>o</u>int

A toast

B enjoy

C ocean

D praise

9 <u>ch</u>est

A ticket

B fence

C cellar

D pinch

10 cr<u>y</u>ing

A very

B crayon

C polite

D yellow

11 Read the sentence below.

Jack packed all of his clothes in the black backpack for the trip.

Which word family do most of the words in this sentence belong to?

A -in

B -or

C -ack

D -all

12 Which of these words is in the same word family as *light*?

A fright

B kite

C school

D ball

13 Read the sentence below.

The cardinal is Indiana's state bird.

Which of these words from the sentence has four syllables?

A state

B cardinal

C bird

D Indiana

Word Parts

Prefixes, Suffixes, and Root Words

Many words are made up of different parts. A word may have a **prefix,** a **root word,** and a **suffix.** If you know what some or all of the parts mean, you can figure out the meaning of the word.

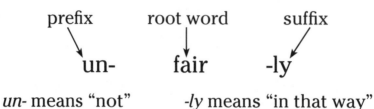

prefix   root word   suffix

un-   fair   -ly

un- means "not"   *-ly* means "in that way"

So, the word *unfairly* means "not in a fair way."

Prefixes

A **prefix** is a word part added to the beginning of the word. A prefix changes the meaning of the root word to make a new word. The prefix *un-* means "not." If you add *un-* to the word *kind,* you make a new word that means "not kind."

Prefix Chart

Prefix	Meaning	Example
dis-	not, opposite	disappear
in-	in, not	inactive
pre-	before	preschool
re-	back, again	replay
un-	not	unpleasant

Match a prefix with each of these root words to make a word that fits the new meaning.

Prefix	Root Word	New Meaning	New Word
	paid	paid before	
	agree	not agree	
	turn	turn back	

Guided Practice

Answer the following questions.

What is the root word of *unusually?*

   A usually

   B unusual

   C usual

   D unused

> You know that *un-* is a prefix and *-ly* is a suffix. If you take them away, the root word is left. So the correct answer is *usual,* choice C.

The word *inexpensive* means

   A not costly

   B high priced

   C very valuable

   D more expensive

> Because the prefix *in-* means "not" and *expensive* means "costly," *inexpensive* means "not costly." Choice A is correct.

The word *dishonest* means

A honest before

B not honest

C honest again

D too honest

You know that the prefix *dis-* means "not" or "opposite." Someone who is *dishonest* is not honest. The correct answer is choice B.

Suffixes

A **suffix** is a word part added to the end of the word. Like a prefix, a suffix changes the meaning of a word.

All players trying out for the team will be treated *fairly*.

You know what *fair* means. The suffix *-ly* means "like" or "in that way." *Fairly* means "in a fair way."

Some suffixes change words to different parts of speech. When you add the suffix *-ly* to the adjective *fair*, you make the adverb *fairly*.

Suffix Chart

Suffix	Meaning	Example
-able	able to be	breakable
-er	one who does something	singer
-ful	full of, likely to	peaceful
-less	without	fearless
-ness	quality or state of	kindness

Match a suffix with each of these root words to make a new word that fits the new meaning.

Root Word	Suffix	New Meaning	New Word
thought		without thinking	
spread		able to be spread	
good		state of being good	
teach		one who teaches	
joy		full of joy	

Guided Practice

Answer the following questions.

What is the root word of *disagreeable?*

  A disagree

  B agree

  C agreeable

  D agreement

Without the prefix *dis-* and the suffix *-able,* you have the root word *agree.* Choice B is the correct answer.

The word *performer* describes

  A one who performs

  B the state of performing

  C able to perform

  D likely to perform

The suffix *-er* means "one who does something." Try to use the word in a sentence. *(Alex is a circus performer.)* The correct answer is choice A.

The word *helpful* means

A   a person who helps

B   a state of helping

C   able to help

D   full of help

Because the suffix -*ful* means "full of," *helpful* must mean "full of help," or "ready to help." The correct answer is choice D.

More Ways to Make Words

A **compound word** is made up of two smaller words. The words that make up a compound word can stand alone, unlike prefixes or suffixes.

You can make several compound words with the word *back*: *backboard, background, backyard, backpack,* and *backbone.* If you don't know what a compound word means, you can try to figure out its meaning from the words that make up the compound word.

Here are some compound words that you probably know.

WORD		WORD		COMPOUND WORD
home	+	work	=	homework
play	+	ground	=	playground
wind	+	shield	=	windshield
bee	+	hive	=	beehive
snow	+	flakes	=	snowflakes
summer	+	time	=	summertime

Draw a line to connect each part of a compound word. Then write the word on the line.

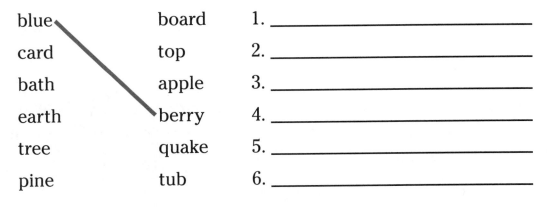

blue   board   1. _____

card   top   2. _____

bath   apple   3. _____

earth   berry   4. _____

tree   quake   5. _____

pine   tub   6. _____

A **contraction** is two words written together as one word with one or more letters left out. An apostrophe (') takes the place of the missing letter or letters.

is not → isn't	was not → wasn't	do not → don't
are not → aren't	were not → weren't	I am → I'm
I will → I'll	that is → that's	cannot → can't

Guided Practice

Read the passage. Then answer the questions that follow.

It's noon. Tina is hungry. She and her <u>classmates</u> walk to the cafeteria. Tina gets in line and takes a tray and silverware. Today, she chooses a salad, a sandwich, applesauce, a cupcake, and a milkshake. As she gets to the end of the line, she reaches into her pocket for her lunch money.

"Oh, no!" cries Tina to the cashier. "My lunch money is gone!"

Which two words make up the contraction *It's* in sentence 1?

A I will

B It is

C I am

D It will

Remember that a contraction is two words written together with an apostrophe taking the the place of a missing letter or letters. You can tell that *It's* is a contraction for *It is,* choice B.

Which of the following compound words names something you can drink?

A silverware

B milkshake

C applesauce

D cupcake

Look at the two words that make up each of the compound words for a clue. You know that milk is something to drink. This tells you that *milkshake,* choice B, is the correct answer.

Classmates are all the students

A in a school

B in a grade

C in a class

D in a community

The clue in the word *classmates* is the word *class.* It tells you that *classmates* are all the students in a class. The correct answer is choice C.

Test Yourself

Read the story. Then answer the questions that follow.

Alandra read her mom's note: *Please close the windows before you leave for the ballpark.* Alandra <u>recalled</u> that the weatherman said to expect a thunderstorm. She quickly glanced outside. The sun was shining. The sky was absolutely <u>cloudless</u>. It was a beautiful morning. A storm seemed unlikely, so she left the windows open.

Alandra grabbed her baseball glove. On her way out, she double-checked the front door. She wanted to make sure it was locked. Then she raced off to meet her friends. About an hour later, Alandra noticed that the wind had picked up and the sun was hidden behind a wall of dark clouds. A bolt of lightning streaked across the sky. Then a <u>thunderclap</u> startled the <u>ballplayers</u>. Suddenly, Alandra remembered the note she had ignored. She knew how <u>displeased</u> her mother was going to be. "Hey, guys," she yelled to her friends, "I've got to get home before it starts raining! See you later."

1 The word *cloudless* means

A clear

B cloudy

C full of clouds

D slightly cloudy

2 A *thunderclap* is

   A the sound made by clapping hands

   B the loud sound made by thunder

   C the sound made by the wind

   D the sound made by lightning

3 The word *displeased* means

   A able to please

   B one who is pleased

   C not pleased

   D very pleased

4 The word *ballplayers* describes

   A a game that is played

   B a place to play ball

   C the ball that is played with

   D those who play ball

5 In this story, *recalled* means

   A called back to mind

   B ordered back

   C called over again

   D called ahead

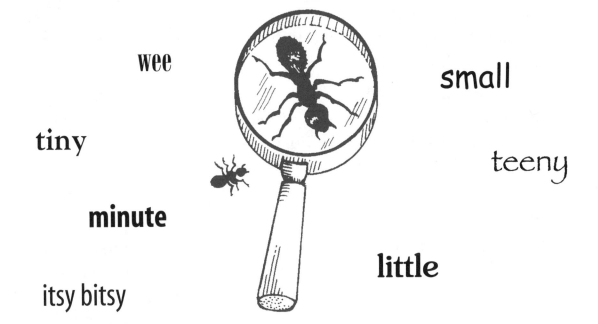

wee

small

tiny

teeny

minute

little

itsy bitsy

Word Clues

Your vocabulary is made up of all the words you know. You use many words when you speak and write. But you know even more words than the ones you use. They are words you understand when you listen or read.

When you read, you probably don't know every word you see. You can often figure out the meaning of a new word from other words near it in a sentence or paragraph.

Juan pushed through the thicket, moving branches aside until he saw daylight and the field at last.

You may know that the word *thicket* means "an area of thick bushes or small trees." If you didn't know the meaning of the word, you could figure it out from the other words and ideas in the sentence. These words are **context clues.** Juan has to push his way out, and he must move branches aside. He is also in a dark place, but there is a field ahead.

Guided Practice

Read the passage. Then answer the questions that follow.

If you go to the children's section of the library, you are sure to find books with <u>illustrations</u> by Brian Pinkney. Brian draws and paints pictures for books. He is an illustrator. Maybe you have read *Cosmo and the Robot, JoJo's Flying Side Kick,* or *Max Found Two Sticks.*

Brian's mother writes children's books, and his father is an illustrator. When Brian was growing up, he often watched his father work in his art studio. Brian began to draw as a <u>youngster</u>. He was just 4 or 5 at the time. To encourage Brian's drawing, his parents created an art studio for him in a walk-in closet.

When he was in school, Brian often did illustrations to earn extra credit for school projects. In history classes, he learned about <u>prominent</u> people. He read about Benjamin Banneker, Duke Ellington, and Martin Luther King. They were famous and important. And they were African Americans, like him. Later, Brian's wife Andrea wrote books about some of these famous people. Brian drew the pictures for her books. He also illustrates books by other authors and draws pictures for books he writes himself.

The word *illustrations* means

A words

B readings

C pictures

D feelings

Sentence 2 says that Brian Pinkney draws and paints pictures for books. *Illustrations* are pictures that go with stories or articles. The answer is choice C.

26

A *youngster* is

    A a young artist

    B a young boy or girl

    C a newborn boy

    D the parent of a young child

> The word *young* in *youngster* is a clue. So is sentence 4 of paragraph 2. It states that Brian was 4 or 5 at the time he started to draw, so he was just a child. The correct choice is B.

Prominent means

    A strong   **C** illustrator

    B older   **D** well known

> The two sentences that follow the word *prominent* tell the names of people and contain the phrase *famous* and *important*. These clues tell you *prominent* means "well known." The correct choice is D.

Synonyms and Antonyms

Synonyms and **antonyms** are two specific types of context clues. Synonyms are words that mean the same, or almost the same, like the words at the top of page 25. They are all synonyms you can use to describe something very small.

Look for a pair of synonyms in this sentence.

> Maria will attempt the long jump, and Rory will try to run a mile.

If you did not know the word *attempt,* you could figure it out from the synonym *try* in the second part of the sentence. If you exchange the synonyms, the sentence will have the same meaning.

Antonyms are words that mean the opposite. Look for a pair of antonyms in this sentence.

> Max broke a wing on his model airplane, but he repaired it with some glue.

The words *broke* and *repaired* are antonyms. The word *but* is a signal. It tells you that repairing something is the opposite of breaking it.

Guided Practice

Choose the best word to complete each sentence.

To be *certain* is to be

A shy

B afraid

C eager

D sure

If you know the answer to a question is correct, you might say that you are *certain*. *Sure* is a good synonym for *certain*, so choice D is correct.

A *basin* is a

A sink

B game

C spice

D barrel

When you wash your hands, the water flows from the faucet into a *basin*. A basin is a *sink*, choice A.

The opposite of *ashamed* is

A sad

B proud

C embarrassed

D frightened

You might be *ashamed* to tell your parents that you did poorly on a test. If you do well on a test, then you would most likely feel the opposite of *ashamed*, or *proud*. So the best answer is choice B.

Words with Multiple Meanings (Homographs)

Some words have multiple, or many, meanings. A dictionary lists each meaning separately, sometimes with a number in front. These words are known as homographs: Words that are spelled the same but have different meanings. The word *fair* has more than one meaning. Here are some meanings of the word *fair*.

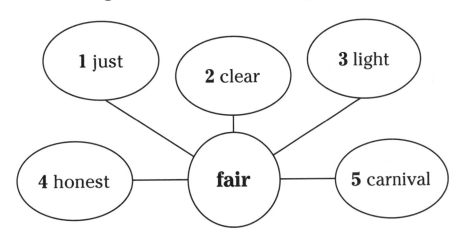

How can you tell which meaning of *fair* is correct when you read? One thing you can do is to look for clues in the sentence.

The baby has blue eyes and *fair* hair.

Which word from the word web could you use in place of *fair* in this sentence? The only word with the same meaning is *light*.

Write the correct meaning of *fair* for each sentence. Use the meanings in the word web.

Sentence	Meaning
Ann rode the Ferris wheel twice at the **fair.**	
Madison is known for playing **fair.**	
Do you think Mr. Lee is a **fair** judge?	
The forecast calls for **fair** weather tomorrow.	

The word *lead* also has multiple meanings. "The toy soldiers are made of *lead.*" *Lead* means the material the soldiers are made of. In the sentence "He is in the *lead,*" *lead* means to be in the front.

Homophones

Homophones are words that sound alike but have different spellings and meanings.

Homophone Chart

for four (4)	What did Ben have **for** breakfast? He had **four** pancakes, some bacon, and juice.
there their they're	**There** are two new boys in our class. **Their** family moved to our town. **They're** twins and they look alike.
to too (also) two (2)	Jason gave a dollar **to** his little sister Olivia. Emily gave her a dollar, **too.** Now Olivia has **two** dollars.

Use the homophones from the chart above to finish the sentences.

1 My friends said _____ going to the mall with _____ parents and

should be _____ by noon.

2 Adam has _____ much homework, so he can't go _____ the

game with us at _____ o'clock.

3 Jackson and Pedro said the gift _____ Mike cost eight dollars, so they

each gave _____ dollars to pay for it.

Guided Practice

Read the poem. Then answer the questions that follow.

Mary had a little lamb,
    Its fleece was white as snow,
And everywhere that Mary went
    The lamb was <u>sure</u> <u>to</u> go.

It followed her <u>to</u> school one day,
    Which was against the <u>rule</u>;
It made the children laugh and <u>play</u>
    <u>To</u> see a lamb at school.

Read this dictionary entry.

> **rule n. 1.** authority, government
> **2.** law **3.** habit, custom **4.** thin
> metal strip to print lines

Read these lines from the poem.

> *It followed her to school one day,*
> *Which was against the <u>rule</u>;*

Which meaning of *rule* is used in the sentence?

  A definition 1

  B definition 2

  C definition 3

  D definition 4

In the poem, *rule* means "a law about how to behave." Choice B is the correct answer.

Which sentence uses the homophone *to* the same way as in the poem?

A We all wanted to go to the park.

B There are two children in my family.

C Those shoes are too small for my feet.

D My sister needs new shoes, too.

The homophone *to* is used three times in the poem. It does not mean "also," and it is not used as the number "two." The answer is choice A.

In which sentence does the word *sure* mean the same as it means in the poem?

A He kept a sure hold on the dog's leash.

B The fastest car is sure to win the race.

C Sure enough, the mail came late again.

D I know for sure I locked the door.

In choice A, *sure* means "firm." Sure enough (choice C) means "as expected." In choice D, *sure* means "without a doubt." But in the poem, *sure* means "something that is bound to happen." The lamb was *sure* to follow Mary everywhere. The only sentence that uses *sure* that way is choice B, so B is the correct answer.

Test Yourself

Read the story. Then answer the questions that follow.

The Lion and the Mouse

One day, a lion was napping in the tall grass. A <u>timid</u> mouse came along. It didn't notice the lion and ran over its nose. The lion awakened and <u>snatched</u> the poor mouse.

"Let me go," begged the <u>terrified</u> little mouse. "If you do, one day I will repay you."

The lion roared with laughter. How could a little mouse help him? He decided to <u>release</u> the mouse anyway.

A week later, the lion became entangled in a hunter's net. Because it couldn't get free, the angry lion roared and roared. It could be heard from almost two miles away. The mouse knew the voice and soon found the lion. It bit and chewed at the ropes. Before <u>long</u>, it had freed the grateful lion.

1 The opposite of *timid* is

A bold

B tiny

C shy

D sharp

2 The word *snatched* means

A watched

B grabbed

C scared

D pushed

3 To be *terrified* means to be

    A startled

    B amused

    C amazed

    D frightened

4 The word *release* means the opposite of

    A eat

    B free

    C catch

    D stay

5 In which sentence does the word *long* mean the same as it does in the last sentence of the story?

    A We long to take a vacation.

    B Our table is 32 inches wide and 72 inches long.

    C We just finished reading a long story.

    D Summertime will be here before long.

6 Which sentence uses the same homophone as in paragraph 4 of the story?

    A The faucet had a leak.

    B Julie was sick, and too weak to play in the soccer game.

    C The family's dog had been missing for a week.

    D Greg liked to wreck his toy truck into a tree.

Rules of English

Standards 3.6.2–8

The English language has rules. Some rules apply to both speaking and writing. For example, you say or write, "I ate an apple," not "Me eat a apple." Other rules apply only to writing, such as using a capital letter at the beginning of a sentence. You might not think much about these rules when you read. But knowing and using the rules of English will help you to say what you mean when you speak and write.

Parts of Speech

Words do different jobs. Some words *name,* some *do,* others *describe* or tell about something. Words are grouped into **parts of speech** depending on the jobs they do.

A **noun** is a word that names a person, place, or thing. A **proper noun** is the name of a certain person, place, or thing. Proper nouns always begin with a capital letter. Other nouns do not begin with a capital letter unless they are at the beginning of a sentence.

Nouns:	girl	city	pet
Proper nouns:	Kate	Fort Wayne	Fluffy

A **pronoun** takes the place of a noun in a sentence.

She went home.	**I** saw **her** yesterday.	**We** left early.
It is in the car.	Ace is **his** dog.	**He** will call **you.**

A **verb** is an action word. Some verbs are called **being verbs** because they describe a "state of being."

Action verbs:	sit	stand	run	walk
Being verbs:	is	are	was	were

Verbs are grouped in **tenses,** depending on whether the action is in the past, present, or future.

Past tense:	thought	was	danced	climbed
Present tense:	think	is	dance	climb
Future tense:	will think	will be	will dance	will climb

An **adjective** is a word that describes a noun.

a **big** apple	a **tall** man	a **blue** bird
many people	**fast** runners	**sunny** days

An **adverb** is a word that tells *how, where,* or *when* and often describes a verb. Adverbs also describe adjectives. Many adverbs end in *-ly.*

She ran **quickly.**	Rain fell **softly.**	I played **well.**
He smiled **proudly.**	I **always** run **fast.**	**Today** I did my best.

Sometimes the same word may be used as a different part of speech in a different sentence.

Let's **fish** in this lake.	(verb)
I caught a **fish!**	(noun)
I can **run** fast.	(verb)
My best **run** was last week.	(noun)
I **dream** of running races.	(verb)
My **dream** is to win first place.	(noun)

Guided Practice

Answer the following questions.

Read the sentence below.

> *Did you hear the dog <u>bark</u>?*

In this sentence, what part of speech is the word *bark?*

    A noun

    B verb

    C adjective

    D adverb

> *Bark* can be a noun: "The bark of the tree is rough." But in this sentence, *bark* is an action word. It's a verb that tells what the dog did. Choice B is correct.

Read the sentence below.

> *Grandma is always <u>kind</u> and gentle.*

In this sentence, the word *kind* is

    A a noun

    B a verb

    C an adjective

    D an adverb

> *Kind* can be used as a noun or an adjective. You could add *-ly* to make an adverb, *kindly.* But in this sentence, *kind* is used to describe Grandma. It is an adjective, so choice C is correct.

Capital Letters

In English, you use capital letters for

- the first letter of any sentence.

My address was written on the letter.

- the first letter of any proper noun that names a certain person, place, or thing.

James **S**mith, 104 **B**road **S**treet, **C**olumbus, **I**ndiana

- the first letter in relationship words or titles if they are used before or in place of a name.

I asked **D**ad if we could visit **A**unt **J**ulie.
Mrs. **P**age said that **D**r. **W**hite could see me today.

- the word *I*.

I will see what **I** can do for you.

- the first letter of the first word and of each main word of a title of a book or film.

Talking Walls, by Margy Burns Knight

- the first letter of the names of days and months, but not seasons.

It's **S**aturday, **D**ecember 22, 2009.
Today is the first day of **w**inter.

- the first letter of a holiday

New **Y**ear's **E**ve   the **F**ourth of **J**uly

- the first letter of a period in history

the **Civil War**

Guided Practice

Answer the following questions.

Read the sentence below.

I will ask Uncle Tim to read A <u>Tall</u> Tale *to me.*

Why does the word *Tall* begin with a capital letter?

A It is a proper noun.

B It is part of a title of a book.

C It is the first letter of a sentence.

D It is the first letter of a relationship word.

Tall is not a proper noun, a relationship word, or the first letter of this sentence. But it is a main word in a title of a book, so choice B is the correct answer.

Read the sentence below.

Does Mr. Steven Long live at 86 Straight street?

Which word in the sentence is NOT capitalized correctly?

A Mr.

B Long

C live

D street

Mr. is a title. *Long* is a proper noun, so it should be capitalized. *Street* is also a proper noun in this sentence. It is part of the name of a street, so it should begin with a capital letter. Choice D is correct.

Subjects and Predicates

Every sentence has two parts: a **subject** and a **predicate.** The subject is what (or whom) the sentence is about. The predicate tells something about the subject. In the sentences below, the subject is shown in **bold type,** and the predicate is underlined.

Whitney ran.
The bird flew away.
Dad is working.

Did you notice something about all those sentences? The subjects all have at least one noun. The predicates all have at least one verb. A **complete sentence** is one that has at least one noun as its subject and one verb as its predicate. The following are not complete sentences.

A girl in my class   (missing a predicate)
Comes from Indiana   (missing a subject)

In every sentence, the subject and verb should agree. Verbs like *am, is,* and *was* are used with singular nouns. *Are* and *were* are used with nouns that are plural (naming more than one). For example, *Dad are working* is not a correct sentence, because Dad is a singular noun (naming one person). But *The men are working* is a correct, complete sentence. Another example would be *The boys are going to the party.* This is correct because the noun and the verb are plural. The sentence *The boys is going to the party* is incorrect because it uses a singular verb with a plural noun. If you are not sure whether a sentence is correct, try reading it aloud— or read it silently to yourself if you are taking a test. A sentence that has a subject and verb that don't agree will sound strange.

Guided Practice

Answer the following questions.

Which of the following is a complete sentence?

   A   Mom drove the bus.   **C**   My sister and I.

   B   Stopped at our house.   **D**   Got to school in time.

> The answer is choice A. It is the only choice with a subject *(Mom)* and a predicate *(drove the bus).* Choices B and D are missing a subject, and choice C is missing a predicate.

Which of the following is NOT a correct sentence?

   A   I am going to the store.

   B   My brother are going with me.

   C   We are riding our bikes.

   D   My friend will meet us at the store.

> When you read all four sentences carefully, you can see that choices A, B, and D have singular subjects. Choice C has a plural subject. Which sentence has a subject and verb that do not agree? Choice B is the one that is not a correct sentence.

End Marks and Commas

     End marks come at the end of a sentence. They can be as important as words in reading and writing. End marks help the reader figure out the meaning of a sentence.

     A **statement** is a sentence that tells. It ends with a **period** (.).

> I went to the dentist.
> His office is a busy place.

A **question** is a sentence that asks. It ends with a **question mark (?)**.

> When did you go to the dentist?
> What did he do to your teeth?

An **exclamation** is a sentence that shows surprise, excitement, or other strong feelings. It ends with an **exclamation point (!)**.

> What a nice surprise!
> I can hardly wait!
> Let's go to the party now!

A **command** is a sentence that tells someone to do something. The subject of a command is often not stated, but it is understood to be "you." A command usually ends with a period (.). It may end with an exclamation point (!) if it shows surprise or other strong feeling.

> Put the bag by the door.
> Watch out!
> Call the police!

A **comma (,)** is never used at the end of a sentence. Some of the ways commas are used in a sentence are to

• separate items in a series.

> The salad had lettuce, tomatoes, and carrots in it.

• separate the date and the year.

> I was born on October 5, 2000.

• separate the name of a city from the name of a state.

> Gary, Indiana   Chicago, Illinois

• separate the street address from the city

428 Apple Way, Indianapolis

When the names of cities and states are used in sentences, a comma also separates the name of the state from the rest of the sentence.

People go to Sun Valley, Idaho, to ski.

Guided Practice

Answer the following questions.

Read the sentence below.

Go outside until I call you

What end mark does this sentence need?

A period

B comma

C question mark

D exclamation point

This one is a bit tricky. A period or an exclamation point could be used at the end of this sentence. In a story, you would have to read the other sentences to decide for sure. If something exciting was happening, such as a fire or fire drill, this sentence should end with an exclamation point. Otherwise, a period would be fine. So the answer is choice A or D.

Read the sentence below.

My three dogs are named Rex Max and Sammy.

This sentence needs commas

A before Rex and Max

B after Rex and Max

C before Max and Sammy

D after Max and Sammy

This sentence has three items in a series: the names of three dogs. Put the two commas where they belong before you choose the answer. Here's how the sentence should look: *My three dogs are named Rex, Max, and Sammy.* Choice B is the correct answer.

Test Yourself

Read the passage. Then answer the questions that follow.

Some of My Favorite Books

by Amanda Reilly

Last winter I read a really funny book. It was during the week of February 13, 2008. We had a snowstorm that week. The book was called *Beezus and Ramona* by Beverly Cleary.

Beezus

Beezus always has to take care of her little sister Ramona. Everything Ramona does annoys Beezus, just like everything my little sister does annoys me. People say I shouldn't mind. I say, "Give me a break!"

Ramona

The Beezus and Ramona story is really good. Even though it is fiction. The things in it could happen in real life. I also read *The Hobbit* by J.R.R. Tolkien. It is a fiction book about make-believe creatures who live in a make-believe land. Make-believe things are okay sometimes. But I would rather read books with real facts in them. *Great Pets!* by Sara Stein is my favorite nonfiction book.

Me

My little Sister Teeny

1 Read the sentence from the passage.

It was during the week of February 13, 2008.

Why is there a comma in this sentence?

A to show the end of the sentence

B to show surprise and excitement

C to separate the date and year

D to separate words in a series

2 Read the sentence from the passage.

We had a snowstorm that week.

What is the subject of this sentence?

A We

B had

C snowstorm

D week

3 Read the sentence from the passage.

People say I shouldn't mind.

What part of speech is the word *mind?*

A adjective

B adverb

C noun

D verb

4 Read the sentence from the passage.

I say, "Give me a break!"

This sentence ends with an exclamation point because it

A is asking a question

B shows strong feelings

C lists items in a series

D is not a complete sentence

5 Which of these is NOT a complete sentence?

A Even though it is fiction.

B The story is really good.

C The things in it could happen in real life.

D I also read *The Hobbit*.

6 The first letters of the words *Great Pets!* are capital because they are the first letters of

A a sentence

B relationship words

C words in a book's title

D proper nouns that name things

Most of the reading you do is for information. The lessons in this unit will teach you important skills that will help you read and understand this kind of text. You can use the skills in these lessons to answer test questions, and in all the reading you do.

5 Text Features   Books have organizational features that help you find information. Most things you read also have special text features such as maps, charts, and graphs. This lesson will show how all these features of print help you understand what you read.

6 Sequence   This lesson will help you follow the sequence—the order in which things happen—in what you read.

7 Prior Knowledge and Predictions Prior knowledge is what you already know. Good readers put together what they already know with clues they find in the text to predict what an article will be about. This shows that you understand and can follow what you are reading. This lesson will show you how to use your prior knowledge and experience to understand what you read and make predictions.

8 Inferences and Conclusions Sometimes you have to put together details in a text with what you already know to make inferences and draw conclusions.

9 Main Idea and Details   Finding the main idea is one of the most important skills. This lesson will show you how to find the main idea and know which details support it.

10 Problem and Solution   When you solve a problem, you have found the solution. This lesson will help you learn how to identify the problem and solution.

11 Cause and Effect   Learning to find the causes for why things happen will help you to better understand what you are reading. This lesson will help you find causes and effects.

12 Fact and Opinion   An important part of reading is knowing when an author is giving an opinion instead of straight facts. A fact can be proven. An opinion is what someone thinks or believes; it is neither true nor false. This lesson will help you tell the difference between facts and opinions.

Text Features

Standard 3.2.1

A book is divided into chapters. A table of contents at the front helps you find the chapters. The title page tells you the name of the book and the author. Headings in bold type tell you about what follows. Some books also have a glossary and an index at the back. A glossary has definitions of hard or unusual words. Sometimes you can tell which words will be in the glossary because they appear in bold text. An index lists topics in alphabetical order, with page numbers that tell you where in the text you can find this topic. When you are reading a book, all these **organizational features** can help you find the information you need.

Almost everything you read also has special **text features** that make information clearer.

Photos and their captions can help make the subject clearer.

Headings in **large bold type,** all CAPITALS, or a different **font** tell you the title of a section so you know what information follows.

~~~~~~
~~~~~~
~~~~~~

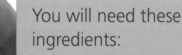

You will need these ingredients:
• wheat toast
• creamy peanut butter
• grape jelly

Numbers or special symbols call your attention to items on a list.

Charts, tables, graphs, and maps can offer valuable examples that help you understand what you're reading.

Guided Practice

Read this title page and table of contents from a book about birds.
Then answer the questions.

Birds

by Arthur North

Table of Contents

In which chapter would you MOST LIKELY find information about how birds build their nests?

A Chapter 1

B Chapter 2

C Chapter 3

D Chapter 4

Look for words in the table of contents that are the same as the topic. Notice the word *nests* in the question. Chapter 2 includes the word *nesting,* so this chapter is most likely to tell about how birds build their nests. Choice B is correct.

Which is the BEST place to look to see if the book tells about penguins?

A title page

B table of contents

C glossary

D index

The title page includes the name of the book and the name of the author. It does not list the topics in the book. The table of contents lists the names of each chapter. Unless there is an entire chapter about penguins, this page will not help you. The glossary has definitions of hard or unusual words. That is not what you are looking for either. Remember that the index includes a list of topics. That is the best place to look to see if the book tells about penguins. Choice D is the correct answer.

If you wanted to learn how a baby bird gets out of its egg, you would look in the chapter that starts on page

A 3

B 9

C 13

D 17

Look for words in the table of contents that are the same as the topic. Notice the word *egg* in the question. Chapter 3 also has the word *egg*, so this chapter is most likely to tell about how a baby bird gets out of its egg. The table of contents tells you that this chapter begins on page 13. So choice C is correct.

Read this passage from a book about birds. Then answer the questions.

Chapter 4
Migration Patterns

Many birds **migrate** from one place to another to look for food or to find a good place to nest. They may stay in one place all summer. Then, when winter is coming, they fly south to where it is warmer. They stay at their warm "winter home" until it is time to fly north to their "summer home."

Geese have the same migration pattern each year. Their summer home is a cooler place like Alaska. When the weather starts to turn cold, they fly south. They spend the winter months in the southern part of the United States and in Mexico.

What is the MOST LIKELY reason the word *migrate* appears in bold?

A to tell readers that the word is in the index

B to tell readers that the word is in the glossary

C to tell readers that the word is in another chapter

D to tell readers that the word is in the table of contents

Words that are in the glossary often appear in bold text. Choice B is the correct answer.

Look at the map below.

Migration of the White-Fronted Goose

How does this map help you understand the migration pattern of geese?

   A It shows where the geese live in the fall.

   B It shows how high most geese fly.

   C It shows the path the geese fly.

   D It shows how cold Alaska is.

The map doesn't mention anything about the temperature of Alaska (choice D) or the height of the geese (choice B). Although it shows you where the geese live in the summer and winter, it's not clear where they live in the fall (choice A). Choice C is the answer you want.

Which photograph BEST matches the information in the passage?

A

A mother bird feeds its young

B

A flock of geese in flight

_____

_____

_____

_____

_____

_____

This kind of question is called a short-response question. Instead of choosing from among four possible answers, you have to write an answer in your own words. Here is a sample answer:

Photo **A** shows a bird feeding its young. This does not go with the information in the text. Photo **B** shows geese flying. This goes with the information in the text. So, photo **B** best matches the information in the passage.

Test Yourself

Read this article. Then answer the questions.

Indiana Dunes National Lakeshore

Indiana Dunes is a very interesting place to visit. It is a state park and a national lakeshore on the southern edge of Lake Michigan. Here you can see changes brought about by the Ice Age. Unexpected features and plants can be found here.

Each year many visitors come to the park.

Mt. Baldy

One of the main attractions is Mt. Baldy. This sand dune is more than a hundred feet tall. Visitors like to hike to the top of the dune to take in the view. On a clear day you can see the Chicago skyline. Scientists call Mt. Baldy a "living dune." Why? The sand dune walks. Actually, it doesn't walk, but it does move. Every year it moves inland four or five feet. The northwest winds move the sand when their wind speeds are above 7 miles per hour.

Listen as you walk on the sand, and you'll hear it sing. The moisture from the water, quartz crystals in sand, and the pressure and friction from your feet walking on the sand create a clear ringing sound. Indiana Dunes is one of only a few beaches in the world where this unusual event occurs.

> **Things to Do**
> - swim at one of the eight beaches
> - cross-country ski or snowshoe on the trails
> - camp inside the park
> - bike along the trails
> - birdwatch

National Natural Landmarks

The park is located along the shores of Lake Michigan. You expect to see a beach here. But would you expect to see a prairie? You will if you walk farther inland. The park is home to a rare tall-grass prairie.

There are other interesting plants here. This is one of the few places you can see arctic and desert plants growing in the same place. The Arctic bearberry is an arctic plant found in the park, and the prickly pear cactus is a desert plant that lives in the dry sandy soil found here.

The Dunes and the prairie are two of the four National Natural Landmarks within the park. Pinhook Bog and Cowles Bog are the other two.

The Pinhook Bog is Indiana's only true bog. A bog is an area of soft, spongy ground that receives freshwater only from rain. This causes the water to be very acidic. Pinhook Bog has some unusual plants. Moss floats on top of the bog. Cranberries and blueberries grow here. You'll also see orchids and an insect-eating plant called a pitcher plant.

You can see many different birds as you walk on the trails. More than 350 different types of birds can be seen in the park. You'll see chickadees, loons, pelicans, hawks, swans, sandpipers, cranes, ducks, and geese. In March, watch for the Great Blue herons as they return to the more than 100 nests inside the park.

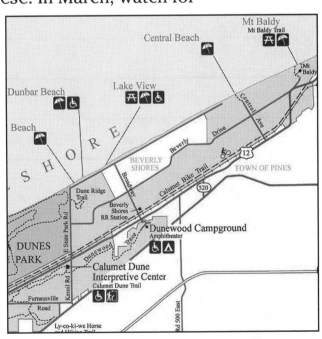

Where Is Indiana Dunes?

Indiana Dunes is located on Indiana State Highway 12. You can get there by car, bus, or train.

Plan Your Visit

The park is open every day. The beaches are open from 7:00 A.M. to dusk. There is no fee unless you are camping or using West Beach.

1 Which text feature in this article is in **bold?**

   A lists

   B pictures

   C captions

   D headings

2 For a list of things to do in Indiana Dunes, you should look

   A under the heading **Where Is Indiana Dunes?**

   B at the caption under the picture

   C in the box

   D at the map

3 How do the text features in the article help you learn about Indiana Dunes? Support your answer with TWO examples of text features.

_____

_____

_____

_____

_____

_____

Sequence

Standards 3.2.7, 3.2.9

In your life, things happen in order.

You get up. → You eat breakfast. → You go to school.

The order in which things happen is called a **sequence.** When you read, you need to follow the sequence of events. Whether you are reading about someone's life, the rules of a game, or directions about how to do something or get somewhere, there is a sequence of events to follow.

Events in reading selections are not always written in order. An author may begin by telling you about something that just happened, and then go back in time to tell about things that happened earlier. Watch for dates and time words, and other clues that can help you put events in order.

Look for sequence words:	
first	recently
second	earlier
third	later
last	finally
next	now
before	after
following	then

Guided Practice

Read this passage from an article. Then answer the questions.

from Make Your Own Weather Station

by Alicia Landry

People use weather stations to collect and record information about the weather. This is how we know what the weather is like at any given time. It also helps people predict the weather.

There are many tools at a weather station. They measure different things. One tells how fast the wind is blowing. Another tells how much rain there was. Others tell how hot or cold it is.

You can make two simple weather station tools yourself. You only need a few things you can find around the house.

A rain gauge tells how much rain fell. You can make a simple rain gauge yourself. All you need is a jar and a ruler. To begin, choose a jar that is the same size at the bottom and the top. It can be made of clear plastic or glass. Put the jar outside. Pick a spot where it is out in the open. After it rains, use the ruler to measure the height of the water in the jar. Now you know how many inches of rain fell.

According to this passage, what do you do AFTER it rains?

A Put the jar outside.

B Make a simple rain gauge.

C Pick a spot where it is out in the open.

D Measure the height of the water in the jar.

Find the phrase *after it rains* in the text. What comes after this? The text says to measure the height of the water in the jar. The correct answer is choice D.

The passage tells you to choose a jar. This happens

A first

B finally

C after it rains

D following all the other events

The passage gives the sequence of events in order. The word *begin* is a clue that something happens first. Choice A is the correct answer.

According to the passage, you use the ruler

A when you pick a spot for the jar   C before it rains

B when you choose a jar   D after it rains

Look for words in the passage that match the words in the question. Then look for clue words that tell when that happened. The clue words *after it rains* go with *use the ruler.* The correct answer is choice D.

Read more of this article. Then answer the questions.

A wind sock tells which direction the wind is blowing. It looks like a big sock blowing in the wind. You may have seen one at a small airport near where you live. You can make your own wind sock, too.

First, take a piece of paper and roll it into a tube. Then tape or glue the paper so it stays that way. Next, cut a second piece of paper into strips. After that, tape or glue the strips to the end of the tube. Last, tie a string to your new wind sock. Then find a place to put it outside. Now you can tell which way the wind is blowing.

According to this passage, what do you do RIGHT BEFORE you tape or glue the strips to the end of the tube?

A Find a place to put it outside.

B Tie a string to your new wind sock.

C Cut a second piece of paper into strips.

D Take a piece of paper and roll it into a tube.

Find in the passage the phrases in the question and answer choices, and then use the clue words to help you. Choices A and B are *last.* Choice D is *first.* The clue words *after that* in front of the phrase that matches the question point you to the right step in the text. Choice C is correct.

If you numbered each step in this passage, which number would go with "tape or glue the paper so it stays that way"?

A 1

B 2

C 3

D 4

That step comes right after the first step, so it is second. Choice B is correct.

Rewrite the directions for making a wind sock as a numbered list.

_____

_____

_____

_____

_____

_____

Look for the sequence words in the article. Here is a sample answer:

1. Take a piece of paper and roll it into a tube.
2. Tape or glue the paper so it stays that way.
3. Cut a second piece of paper into strips.
4. Tape or glue the strips to the end of the tube.
5. Tie a string to your new wind sock.
6. Find a place to put it outside.

Test Yourself

Read this recipe for making cupcakes. Then answer the questions.

Classic Cupcakes

by Lisa Giles

Making cupcakes for the class bake sale is not that hard. You'll need just a few basic things:

- cake mix
- cupcake pan
- paper cupcake liners
- 3 eggs
- 1 cup of milk
- $\frac{1}{2}$ cup oil

After you've gotten everything at the store, find a measuring cup, mixing bowl, and big spoon. Now you're ready to read these directions.

First, preheat the oven to 400 degrees. Then open the cake mix and pour it into a big mixing bowl. Next, crack the eggs into the bowl and add the milk and oil. Then use an electric mixer to blend everything together until the batter is smooth. Finally, pour the batter into the cupcake pans and bake for 30 minutes. Let the cupcakes cool.

1 When do you add the milk and oil?

 A after using the electric mixer

 B after putting the pan in the oven

 C after pouring the batter into the pan

 D after cracking the eggs into the bowl

2 What goes into the mixing bowl FIRST?

    A oil

    B milk

    C eggs

    D cake mix

3 What is the LAST step in the directions?

    A Preheat oven to 400 degrees.

    B Pour the batter into pans.

    C Let the cupcakes cool.

    D Bake for 30 minutes.

4 You should pour the batter into the cupcake pan before you

    A read the directions

    B use the electric mixer

    C put the pan in the oven

    D crack the eggs into the bowl

5 Could the order of the steps for making the cupcakes be changed? Explain why or why not.

_____

_____

_____

_____

_____

Prior Knowledge and Predictions

Standards 3.2.2, 3.2.4

Your mind is busy when you read. You may not be aware of it, but you're always using what you already know to help you understand what you're reading.

Suppose you start reading an article about fish. You already know a lot about fish. You or someone you know may keep fish as pets. You may have seen pictures of different kinds of fish. Maybe you have visited an aquarium. You may know the names of several kinds of fish and a few facts about them. These things are called **prior knowledge.** (*Prior* means "before.") Using prior knowledge can help you understand what you're reading.

As you read, ask yourself questions such as, What do I know about this topic? What do I think about when I look at the title and the pictures? Then use this knowledge as you read.

Before reading the article that starts below, read the title and directions. Then think about your past experiences playing or watching sports. Read the article. Then use your prior knowledge to help you answer the questions that follow.

Guided Practice

Read the first part of an article about a successful female athlete. Then answer the questions.

Call Her Babe

by Nikki Luster

There are many women in sports today. Some play tennis. Some run marathons. Some have won Olympic medals. Today, women play most of the same sports that men do. But this was not always how it was. It was different back in the 1920s and 1930s. Then, girls were not encouraged to do sports. Boys played sports, but not girls. It was rare to find a woman athlete.

One of the first famous women in sports was Babe Didrikson. Her real first name was Mildred. She grew up in Texas. She played a lot of sports as a child. She played baseball with the boys who lived near her. That might explain how she got the nickname "Babe." At that time, Babe Ruth was a famous baseball player. He hit a lot of home runs. Mildred hit a lot of home runs, too.

Why do you think Mildred "Babe" Didrikson played a lot of sports as a child?

A She grew up in Texas.

B She liked playing sports.

C She did not like the name Mildred.

D She was encouraged to play sports.

Choice A is true, but it doesn't explain why Babe played sports. The article says that girls were not encouraged to play sports, so choice D is not the best choice. Choice C may be true, but it is also not the best choice. You know that many people play sports for fun. Choice B is correct.

If you did NOT know where Texas was, you could find out by looking at a

A dictionary

B math textbook

C telephone book

D map of the United States

You know that you use a map to find out where places are. Choice D is correct.

How do you think Mildred felt about the nickname "Babe"?
Use details from the article to support your answer.

_____

_____

_____

_____

_____

_____

Do you have a nickname, or do any of your friends have nicknames? Think about how you feel about your nickname, or about how you think your friends feel about theirs. Here is a sample answer:

> She probably liked her nickname. Babe Ruth was famous and hit a lot of home runs. A nickname like that shows the boys thought she was a good ballplayer like Babe Ruth.

Read more of the article. Then answer the questions.

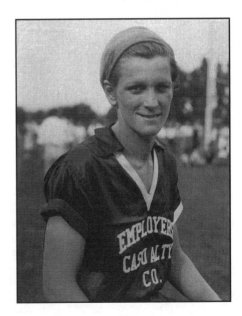

Babe Didrikson played many other sports, too. She was good at all of them. She played basketball. She also played golf. She became a women's golf champion. There is a story that someone once asked Babe if there was anything she didn't play. She answered "dolls."

When she was 21, Babe went to the 1932 Olympic Games. She did three track and field events. She would have done more, but she wasn't allowed. At that time, women were allowed to do only three events at the Olympics.

She won three medals at the Olympics. Two were gold. One was silver. However, not everyone cheered for her. Some people thought that sports should be for men only. Still, Babe did not let other people stop her from doing what she wanted to do with her life. She was proud of herself. She was a good speaker, too. Babe Didrikson was a role model for other women, and helped change the way people thought about women and sports.

What are the Olympic Games?

A video games you play using a computer

B sports contests between people from different countries

C board games that can be played by four or more people

D baseball games where teams of women compete against men

The article tells you that Babe Didrikson won three track and field events at the Olympic Games. Using what you know and what is in the text, you can rule out choices A, C, and D. Choice B is the correct answer.

What are two words that BEST describe Babe Didrikson?

A shy and timid

B tired and lazy

C bold and strong

D angry and unhappy

The article says that Babe Didrikson was proud of herself and that she was a good speaker, too. Nothing in the text supports choices A, B, or D. The correct answer is choice C.

Unit 2 Reading for Information

When you read an article, you think ahead. You make guesses, or **predictions,** about what you read. First, you look at the pictures or other text features and guess what the text might be about. Then as you read you make predictions about what might happen next.

To make a good prediction, you put together clues in the text and what you already know. This helps you understand what you are reading. Making predictions keeps your mind moving forward as you read.

Using a prediction chart is a helpful way to record your predictions as you read.

Text Clues	What I Know	Prediction

Guided Practice

Read this passage which is part of a longer article. Then answer the questions.

There are so many beautiful butterflies and moths. You could spend a whole day just watching butterflies. But if you want to see moths, you have to watch them at night. Some moths are small and brown. Others, such as the luna moth, are big and beautiful. They are interesting to watch.

luna moth

You may think it is hard to see moths or anything else in the dark. That's why you need a light. On a warm summer evening, moths and other bugs will come to a light. You can use any kind of outdoor light. Use a flashlight, a lantern, or an electric light with a long cord.

Sit just far enough away from your light that you can clearly see what comes to it. You will probably see mosquitoes first. Or maybe you will see those tiny flies called gnats. The moths are sure to follow. That is because mosquitoes and gnats are favorite foods for moths.

You can predict that this passage was MOST LIKELY taken from an article about

    A nighttime around the world

    B the life of the monarch butterfly

    C insects with wings

    D insects at night

> Choice C is the correct answer. The clues that help you predict what the whole article is about come from the insects mentioned. Butterflies, moths, gnats, and mosquitoes all have wings. The other answer choices do not include the whole subject of the passage and all the insects mentioned.

What will PROBABLY happen to a mosquito when a moth gets near it?

    A The mosquito will make buzzing sounds.

    B The mosquito will be eaten by the moth.

    C The mosquito will eat the moth.

    D The mosquito will move closer to the light.

> The last sentence tells you that mosquitoes are one of the favorite foods of moths, so you can predict that the moth will probably eat the mosquito. The correct choice is B.

Now read this article about magnets. Then answer the questions that follow.

Exploring Magnets

Have you ever played with a magnet? If you have, then you know that a magnet pulls, or attracts, certain kinds of objects to it. It attracts metal objects made of iron and steel. But a magnet doesn't attract all metal objects. It won't attract objects made of brass or copper. It also won't attract objects made of glass, wood, plastic, or rubber.

A magnet has two poles, the North pole **(N)** and the South pole **(S).** The pull of a magnet is strongest at its poles. The poles on a bar magnet are at each end.

Magnets attract other magnets. This happens when you put the opposite poles near each other. The North and South poles attract each other.

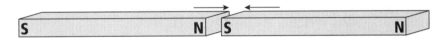

Magnets also push away, or repel, other magnets. This happens when you try to put the same poles together. The North pole of one magnet will repel the North pole of another.

What will happen if you try to put together the South poles of two magnets?

A They will attract each other.

B Nothing will happen.

C They will repel each other.

D First, they will attract each other, and then they will repel each other.

Paragraph 4 explains that when two of the same poles come near each other, the magnets will repel. The picture shows two North poles repelling each other, so you can predict that two South poles would also repel each other. The correct answer is C.

Which one of these objects would a magnet attract?

A a wooden block

B a car key

C a book

D a marble

The third sentence says that a magnet attracts metal objects made of iron or steel. A car key is the only object among the answer choices that is made of metal, so you can predict that a magnet would attract a car key, answer B.

Test Yourself

Now read this article. Answer the questions that follow.

Some people think of Johnny Appleseed as a story character, but he was a real person. His name was John Chapman. He was born in 1774 in Massachusetts.

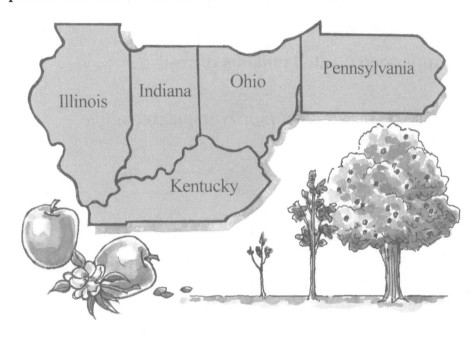

Johnny Appleseed spent 49 years in the wilderness. He planted acres of apple trees. Some of the trees still bear apples. As settlers moved to the wilderness, he sold trees to them. He also gave away trees and seeds. He wanted apple trees to fill the wilderness. Today, that wilderness is Pennsylvania, Ohio, Kentucky, Indiana, and Illinois.

Johnny Appleseed did all the work by himself. He cleared the land. He planted seeds. He built fences to protect the trees. When he traveled, he used a tin pot to gather nuts and berries, carry water and milk, and boil potatoes. Some said that his clothes were made from sacks and that he wore the tin pot on his head. Like many settlers, he also went barefoot.

Johnny Appleseed liked people, and people liked him. As more settlers came, he became a welcomed guest. After each meal, he often told stories or read to them. One night, cattle broke through a fence. He went to help fix it. It was 20 miles away. On the way back, he got sick. Sadly, he did not get better.

1 Which of these statements would be the BEST one to add to the end of the article?

   A   There are many tales about Johnny Appleseed.

   B   John Chapman died at the age of 70, in 1845.

   C   The Johnny Appleseed Festival is held each fall in Fort Wayne, Indiana.

   D   Johnny Appleseed planted millions of seeds.

2 Johnny Appleseed was a real person who planted apple trees in

   A   Canada

   B   Mexico

   C   America

   D   England

3 If you did NOT know where Indiana was, you could find out by looking

   A   in a telephone book

   B   in a dictionary

   C   in a math textbook

   D   on a map of the United States

4 Johnny Appleseed gave seeds and trees to people who were moving

   A   west

   B   east

   C   south

   D   north

5 After reading, you can predict that this passage was MOST LIKELY taken from an article about

    A how to grow apples

    B settlers in the wilderness

    C the eastern United States

    D the life of Johnny Appleseed

6 Which text features BEST help you predict what this article is about?

_____

_____

_____

_____

_____

Inferences and Conclusions

Standards 3.2.3, 3.2.4

A writer does not always tell you everything. Writers want you to figure out some details based on what you know and what you are reading. This is called **making inferences.**

Tara was so excited! This had never happened to her before! As her teammates lifted her on their shoulders, Tara felt so proud. The Tigers had finally won the baseball championship!

The text says:
As her teammates lifted her on their shoulders, Tara felt so proud.

You know:
Players sometimes get carried on their teammates' shoulders when they score winning runs in baseball games.

You can infer:
Tara scored the winning run.

When you put pieces of information together, you are **drawing conclusions.**

An alligator uses its tail to fight. Its tail is a dangerous weapon that can easily break an enemy's bones. A kangaroo uses its tail for balance as it hops along. One type of lizard stores food in its tail.

The passage says:
One animal uses it tail as a weapon. Another uses its tail for balance. Another stores food in its tail.

You can conclude:
Animals use their tails in different ways.

Guided Practice

Read the passage. Then answer the question that follows.

Bats

by Bill Jordan

Are you one of the many people who are afraid of bats? You really shouldn't be, since most kinds of bats are not harmful to people. The old ideas and myths about bats are untrue. Bats are not blind and they don't get tangled in your hair. Sometimes, though, bats do get rabies. This is a deadly disease. So if you ever see a bat on the ground, do not touch it! You should tell an adult right away.

Bats are amazing mammals. If you learn more about them, you may agree. There are about 1,000 kinds of bats. About 70% eat insects. Some insects destroy crops. Other insects, like mosquitoes, are a problem for people and animals. One kind of bat can catch up to 600 mosquitoes in an hour. Imagine what a large group of bats can do! There is a cave in Texas where a colony of over 20 million bats live. In just one night, they eat 250,000 pounds of insects. That's a lot of insects! So, now you understand why bats are valuable.

But wait! There's more. Did you know that bats also play an important role in the survival of rain forests? Some bats eat fruit. While they eat, they drop seeds and spread them. When these seeds fall on the ground, many of them take root. Then new plants grow up. Some bats also help pollinate flowers as they travel from plant to plant, drinking the nectar. In time, the pollinated flowers turn into fruit. Inside the fruit are seeds for new plants. Now you know just a few reasons why bats are amazing!

According to the passage, people should not be afraid of bats. Explain how bats can be useful. Use information from the passage to support your answer.

_____

_____

_____

_____

_____

_____

Paragraphs 2 and 3 of the passage tell that bats eat insects and that they play an important role in the survival of the rain forests. Those two paragraphs explain how bats can be useful. Here is a sample answer:

> Many people are afraid of bats, but there is no need to be. Bats are actually very helpful. Most bats eat insects. Insects can cause big problems for farmers. They destroy crops. Bats help save the crops by eating the insects. Bats also help the rain forests. In the rain forest, the bats help pollinate flowers. They help many new plants grow in the rain forest.

Read the passage. Then answer the questions that follow.

The Colonists and the Powhatans

by Christopher Lansdale

Long ago, a group of about 105 people arrived from England. They started a colony, or settlement, in America. The group included men and seven or eight boys. The boys were about 10 years old.

The colonists landed along the James River. They decided to start a colony there. They named it Jamestown. Most of the men and boys had been wealthy. Back in England, servants did the work for them. In Jamestown, they did not know how to do much for themselves. They did not know how to plant or hunt for food. They built the town on a swamp that had many mosquitoes. Some colonists got sick and died from diseases carried by the mosquitoes.

The American Indians living in the area were known as Powhatans. They could not believe the colonists had chosen such a poor location. They also could not understand why the colonists were starving. There were so many berries, plants, and animals in the forest. The Powhatans tried to help the colonists by giving them food. They had meetings and tried to get along.

Chief Powhatan had many children. But his favorite child was Pocahontas. He thought she was smart. When she was 11 or 12 years old, she was her father's only messenger between the colonists and himself. The name Pocahontas means "joyful one." The name fit her. She was happy and fun loving, and the colonists liked her. She taught the boys how to turn cartwheels.

Some of the young boys spent a month in the Powhatan village. The colonists wanted to show the Powhatans that they trusted them. At times, the colonists and the Powhatans got along very well. At other times, they did not get along. In the end, the colonists and the Powhatans fought bitterly.

What was PROBABLY the reason that the colonists founded Jamestown on a swamp?

    A They had little knowledge of the place.

    B They were sent there by the Powhatans.

    C They thought it would make a good hideout.

    D They thought the water could help the crops grow.

> The passage tells how the colonists did not know how to do much for themselves. It also tells that the Powhatans could not believe that the colonists had chosen such a poor location. This means that when they founded Jamestown, the colonists probably did not know it was a bad spot. Choice A is the correct answer.

Why did the Powhatans have meetings with the colonists?

    A They wanted to live in Jamestown as well.

    B They wanted to be friends with the colonists.

    C They wanted the colonists to go back to England.

    D They wanted the colonists to move away from the swamp.

> The passage tells how the Powhatans helped the colonists. This means that they did not want them to go away. The passage also tells that the Powhatans tried to get along with the colonists. Choice B is correct.

How do you know that Chief Powhatan thought Pocahontas was smart?

A Pocahontas could turn cartwheels.

B Pocahontas's name meant "joyful one."

C Pocahontas made friends with the colonists.

D Pocahontas was his only messenger to the colonists.

> Even though Pocahontas knew how to turn cartwheels and was liked by everybody, those are not the reasons her father thought she was smart. Chief Powhatan trusted his daughter to be his only messenger to the colonists, which showed he thought Pocahontas was smart. Choice D is the correct answer.

After reading the passage, you can conclude that the colonists and the Powhatans

A failed to get along

B never trusted each other

C refused to talk to each other

D fought bitterly from the start

> The last paragraph of the passage tells that, in the end, the colonists and the Powhatans fought bitterly. This means that they failed to get along. Choice A is the correct answer.

Test Yourself

Read the article. Then answer the questions.

Tornadoes Strike Tennessee

On Friday, April 6, 2006, tornadoes swept across the state of Tennessee. Just before 1:30 in the afternoon, a swirling funnel cloud formed outside of Nashville. The tornado first touched down in the city of Charlotte. It continued its path across the state. Then it reached the town of Gallatin. The people in this town felt the tornado's full effect.

The tornado ripped through the town. It flattened neighborhoods and destroyed houses. Trees snapped in two. Telephone poles toppled over. Many places didn't have electricity. The hospitals were filled with people who had been hurt by the storm.

On Saturday, people came out of hiding. Alma Johnson cried when she saw what had happened to her house. Mike Gomez searched through the damage. He found a family picture. He continued searching late into the day. He only found a few more of his family's things.

Tornadoes can be very damaging. There are ways to stay safe, though. Weather forecasters can warn people that a tornado is coming. This gives people time to get to a safe place. People should go to their basements, their closets, or their bathrooms. It is not safe to stand near doors or windows. The most important thing to do is to take tornado warnings seriously. When you hear one, head to safety.

1 You can tell that the tornado was destructive because it

   A   was shaped like a funnel

   B   traveled across the state

   C   touched down in the afternoon

   D   destroyed houses and hurt people

2 Why do you think Alma Johnson cried when she saw her house?

   A   Her house had been destroyed by the storm.

   B   Her house was not harmed by the storm.

   C   She wanted a new house.

   D   She wanted to keep hiding.

3 Why might it be unsafe to stand near a window during a tornado?

   A   You could see the tornado.

   B   You could hear the tornado.

   C   The window might break.

   D   You might get wet from the rain.

4 Based on what happened to Alma Johnson and Mike Gomez, how do tornadoes affect people?

   _____

   _____

   _____

   _____

Standard 3.2.5

Main Idea

Everything you read is *about* something. The **main idea** tells what the whole article is about in a few words or a sentence.

Think of the last book you read. You could probably describe in one or two sentences what it was about—even if it was a long book. It's the same with each chapter in the book. It's even the same with a paragraph. Each one has a **main idea.**

In many paragraphs, there is one sentence that tells the most important idea. It is called the **topic sentence.** It is often the first or last sentence of the paragraph. The other sentences in a paragraph explain the topic sentence.

- To answer a main idea question, look for the answer that tells what the whole article or paragraph is about.

- Some main idea questions ask you to choose a title for the article.

Supporting Details

You know the main idea is what a passage or paragraph is mostly about. **Details** are interesting bits of information that tell more about the main idea. Details can help you see, hear, and feel what you're reading.

Guided Practice

Read this article about forts. Then answer the questions.

Forts Long Ago and Now

by William Jefferies

A fort is a safe place where people can protect themselves. Long ago, there were many castles that were forts. A fort was often one main building with a high wall around it. Guards stood in towers at the corners of the wall. Around the outsides of the wall was a man-made river called a moat. A drawbridge was let down over the moat when people wanted to enter or leave the fort.

Can you guess who is building forts these days? Today, the greatest numbers of forts are built by boys and girls like you. These forts are not built to keep out enemies. Instead, a fort is a special and private place. A person can be alone in the fort. Only invited guests are allowed in. Some kids build forts under tables or behind chairs inside their homes. Other kids build outdoor forts. A big cardboard box makes a nice fort for one or two people. Every kid who wants a special place can make some kind of fort.

Which sentence states the main idea of paragraph 1?

A Long ago, there were many castles that were forts.

B Guards stood in towers at the corners of the wall.

C Around the outsides of the wall was a man-made river called a moat.

D A drawbridge was used to enter or leave the fort.

In many paragraphs, the topic sentence is the first or last sentence, but not in this paragraph. The main idea of the paragraph is castle forts—not guards, moats, or drawbridges. Choice A is the correct answer.

Where can you find the main idea of the whole article?

    A in the title

    B in the last sentence of paragraph 1

    C in the first sentence of paragraph 2

    D in the second sentence of paragraph 2

> Ask yourself which answer choice has a phrase or sentence that describes the whole article. The title gives the main idea, that the article is about forts long ago and now. Choice A is the correct answer.

Fill out the main idea/details chart to show the main idea of the selection and three important details.

Main Idea:_____

_____

Details:

    1._____

    2._____

    3._____

Here is a sample answer:

Main Idea: Forts long ago and now
Details:
    1. Long ago, many castles were forts.
    2. Long ago, forts were built to keep out enemies.
    3. Today, children build forts and invite their friends inside.

Read this article about the Statue of Liberty. Then answer the questions.

Lady Liberty

by Sylvia Fry

The Statue of Liberty is a symbol of America. It was a gift from the people of France to the people of the United States. This famous landmark opened to the public on October 28, 1886. It was an important day in U.S. history. Since then, it has welcomed millions of people to New York Harbor and America.

The idea for the statue started in France. At that time, many French people did not like their government. Some wanted France to be more like the United States. A French man thought of a way to get his people to think more about their freedom. He hoped that this would lead to a better government for France. His idea became the Statue of Liberty.

An artist named Bartholdi [bahr•THOL•dee] designed the statue. He came to America in 1871. At that time, people traveling from Europe to America came by ship. Bartholdi's ship steamed into New York Harbor. It was an exciting time for him. He was on deck looking around. He saw an old fort on an island in the harbor. He knew right away that this was the place for his statue. Everyone who sailed into New York Harbor would see it.

Picking the place to put the statue was the easy part. It cost a lot of money to make something so big. It took a long time for the French people to get enough money to build it. Americans gave money to make the place for it to stand. Finally, it all came together. More than 100 years later, the Statue of Liberty continues to be an important symbol of freedom and independence.

Which of these sentences tells the main idea of paragraph 1?

A The Statue of Liberty is a symbol of America.

B It was a gift from the people of France to the people of the United States.

C This famous landmark opened to the public on October 28, 1886.

D Since then, it has welcomed millions of people to New York Harbor and America.

> The first sentence of paragraph 1 is the topic sentence. It tells the main idea. Choices B, C, and D are supporting details. Choice A is correct.

What is the main idea of paragraph 2? Explain your answer.

_____

_____

_____

_____

_____

_____

> What is the paragraph MOSTLY about? Here is a sample answer:

>> The main idea of paragraph 2 is that the idea for the Statue of Liberty started in France. This main idea is in the first and last sentences of the paragraph. The sentences in the middle of the paragraph are supporting details. They give interesting information about the main idea.

Test Yourself

Read this article about frogs. Then answer the questions.

A lot of people like frogs. There are stories and movies about make-believe frogs that talk and act like people. But real frogs have a real problem. They are dying out.

Frogs are very sensitive to their environment. Water passes through their skin and eggs. This is not a problem if the water is clean. But poisons in bad water can kill frogs. It also hurts their eggs. This is one reason why so many frogs are dying out. There are other reasons, too.

Many frogs live in wetlands. Now, wetlands are disappearing. There are homes and shopping centers where there used to be wetlands. Destroying wetlands destroys frogs. And some of these frogs are very special.

An Australian frog, which is now thought to be extinct, was the only known animal to give birth through its mouth. Baby frogs that did not leave their mother's mouth were swallowed back. They would be born later.

1 Which of these would make the BEST title for this article?

   A Make-Believe Frogs

   B Frogs in Danger

   C Special Frogs

   D Wetlands

2 Which of these tells the main idea of paragraph 1?

   A Frogs are dying out.

   B A lot of people like frogs.

   C Wetlands are disappearing.

   D Make-believe frogs are cute.

3 Which of these is the topic sentence of paragraph 3?

   A Many frogs live in wetlands.

   B Now, wetlands are disappearing.

   C Destroying wetlands destroys frogs.

   D And some of these frogs are very special.

4 What is paragraph 4 all about?

   A a frog's mouth

   B a special frog

   C baby frogs

   D Australia

5 This article explains that frogs are dying out. Include TWO details from the article that support this idea.

_____

_____

_____

_____

_____

_____

Problem and Solution

Sometimes when you read, you are looking for a solution to a problem. First, you need to identify what the problem is. Then you must find a solution that matches the problem. Suppose your feet are hurting. You soon discover the problem: Your shoes are too tight. Your feet have grown since last year when you got those sneakers. When you tell your mom, she says, "Let's go to the mall and buy you some new sneakers this weekend." So you get some new shoes that fit your feet. That's the solution!

Problem

Solution

Guided Practice

Read the article about spending money. Then answer the questions that follow.

Decisions, Decisions, Decisions

Suppose you just received $50 for your birthday. Your parents say you can spend it any way you like. You've wanted a certain game for quite a while. It costs $49.99. But now that you have the money to buy the game, you're not sure what to do. Should you spend the money, or should you save it?

Did you ever think that spending your money would be such a problem? Well, here are some questions to ask yourself and some suggestions to think about. They can help you make a decision when you're thinking about buying something.

$ First, ask yourself this question: Do I really *need* it? Be honest! If your answer is *no,* then answer this question: Do I really *want* it? Please read on.

$ If you buy the item, will you play with it, use it, or wear it? Or, will it end up with other things you just "had to have" and don't use any more? Think about the money you could save.

$ Here's something else to consider. If you spend all your money now, you won't have money for other things you may want or really need later. Can you live without the item for the next few days? If you can, that will give you time to think about your decision and do some checking.

$ If you wait, the item could go on sale. Did you look in the Sunday newspaper? It usually has store ads and flyers about sales for the upcoming week. Who knows? You may see that the item you want is on sale. Wouldn't you be glad you waited?

$ When you decide to buy an item, it's a good idea to think about where to buy it. Are there outlets and discount stores nearby? If so, be sure to check them out. You may be able to buy what you want for much less at a discount store.

$ Think about how you answered all the questions. Now you should be ready to make a decision.

What problem does this article help you solve?

   A how to make a decision about buying something

   B how to earn money for something you want

   C how to save money for something you want

   D how to get your parents to buy what you want

> The article does not tell you how to earn or to save money. It does not suggest that you ask your parents to buy something. Paragraph 1 suggests the problem. The correct answer is choice A—how to make a decision about buying something.

Deciding whether or not to buy something can be a problem. What does the article suggest that you do?

A go ahead and buy what you want

B save your money

C answer some questions first

D ask your parents what they think

Here you are asked to identify the solution. The article does not tell you to buy something, save your money, or ask your parents. Instead, it suggests that you answer some questions and think about suggestions that will help you make a decision. The correct choice is C.

If you spend all your money now, you may not have money later. That's a problem. What should you do?

A Buy it anyway and borrow money later.

B Ask your parents to buy it for you now.

C Wait a few days and think about it.

D Put your money in the bank.

Any one of the choices may solve the problem, but the fifth paragraph holds the correct answer. Choice C is correct. It suggests that if you can wait a few days before buying the item, you'll have time to think about your decision and do some checking.

Now read this news item and answer the questions that follow.

Scientists Solve Mystery

CHEYENNE, WY—The mystery of 300 dead elk has been solved. A lichen that grows in southern Wyoming was responsible for their deaths. Lichen is a mossy plant. It contains an acid. This acid was harmless to the elk that usually live in southern Wyoming. Scientists believe the dead elk were from Colorado. The border of this state is just 50 miles from where the elk died. When these elk ate the lichen, their stomachs could not process the acid. The acid caused their muscle tissue to break down.

Scientists found lichen in the stomachs of the dead elk. That's when they began to suspect that lichen was the cause. They had already ruled out certain diseases and other causes. To be sure, they fed the lichen plants to three elk. These elk got sick and had to be put down.

Scientists still have questions. They want to know why the lichen had so much acid. Did drought conditions have something to do with it? Why hasn't lichen affected the elk before? They must find answers. Then they must find ways to prevent this from happening again.

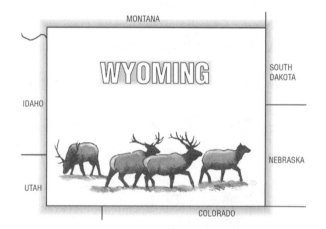

What mystery did scientists solve?

A why lichen had so much acid

B why 300 elk died

C why acid causes muscle tissue to break down

D why elk from Colorado were in Wyoming

Sentence 1 of the news story tells you that the mystery of 300 dead elk has been solved. The correct answer is choice B.

How did the scientists come to suspect that lichen was the problem?

A They knew something similar had happened before.

B They knew lichen had high levels of acid.

C They had ruled out everything else.

D They found lichen in the stomachs of the dead elk.

> The last paragraph of the news story implies that this had not happened before. It's true that the scientists had ruled out just about everything else, but they didn't begin to suspect lichen until they found it in the stomachs of the dead elk. Choice D is the correct answer.

How did the scientists know for sure that lichen caused the deaths of 300 elk? Explain how the scientists solved the problem and what they must do now.

_____

_____

_____

_____

_____

Here is a sample answer:

> Scientists found lichen in the stomachs of the dead elk. They fed lichen to three elk to be sure the lichen killed the elk. The three elk became sick and were put down. Scientists need to find out why the lichen had so much acid and why it affected the elk. Scientists need to prevent this from happening again.

Test Yourself

Read the following biography of a child inventor. Then answer the questions that follow.

Have you ever heard of Chester Greenwood? He grew up in Farmington, Maine. Winters there were—and still are—very long, hard, and cold. As a child, Chester had a big problem. His ears not only got cold in winter, they turned colors. Everyone in the town knew about Chester's red ears.

On his 15th birthday in 1873, Chester received a pair of ice skates. It was winter, so the nearby pond was frozen. Chester decided to try out his skates. But the weather was too cold and windy. He had to turn back and go home.

Chester did not give up. He really wanted to try his new skates. The next day he wrapped a wool scarf around his head. It worked! Chester's ears stayed quite warm. But the wool made his ears so itchy that he soon had to go home again.

Chester had an idea. He gathered what he needed: wire, fur, and some soft velvet material. He used the wire to make loops about the size of his ears. Then he asked his grandmother to sew the velvet to the inside of each loop. He had her sew fur to the outside, for warmth. Chester put the loops over his cap to cover his ears. Then he went outside to test his new cap. He was so excited. His idea worked!

Soon the people of Farmington were noticing Chester's ear flaps instead of his ears. It wasn't long before he and his grandmother were filling orders for the furry flaps. They called them "earmuffs." By 1877, people throughout the area were buying Greenwood's earmuffs. By then, 19-year-old Chester had also made a better design. He was using a flat spring to connect the two flaps. The spring fit over the head and kept the flaps over the ears where they belonged.

Chester Greenwood's business did well. He went on to create a machine to make his earmuffs. He then opened a factory in Farmington. When Chester died in 1937, his earmuff factory was still running.

Today, the people of Maine honor Chester. December 21 is the first day of winter. It is also Chester Greenwood Day.

1 What was Chester's first problem?

A People made fun of his ears.

B Chester couldn't keep his ears warm.

C Chester's ears were too big.

D Chester couldn't buy new ice skates.

2 How did Chester try to solve his problem so he could go skating on the second day?

A He put socks on his ears.

B He pulled his hat over his ears.

C He wrapped a wool scarf around his head.

D He decided not to go ice skating anymore.

3 Chester's solution worked at first, but that created another problem for him. What was this second problem?

A The wool made his ears itchy.

B His ears got too warm.

C The weather was too cold and windy.

D His mother called him home again.

4 Chester finally solved his ear problems by

    A gathering wire, fur, and velvet

    B asking his grandmother for help

    C making furry flaps to wear over his ears

    D calling the furry flaps "earmuffs"

5 By 1877, Chester had improved the design of his earmuffs. Explain the problem he solved by using a flat spring instead of wire.

_____

_____

_____

_____

_____

_____

Cause and Effect

Standard 3.2.8

When you read, you probably see connections between ideas and events. These connections explain why things happen. Your reading makes more sense when you understand these *why* connections. Look for clue words that signal **cause** and **effect.** The thing that happens is the effect. The reason it happens, or what makes it happen, is the cause.

Cause

These clue words signal *causes:*

if, because, since, the reason for

Effect

These clue words signal *effects:*

then, so, as a result, that is why

Sometimes there are no clue words. In that case, ask yourself, Why did this happen? (That's the cause.) Then ask, What happened because of this? (That's the effect.) It might help to add your own clue word (*because* or *so*) when you answer these questions.

Guided Practice

Read this article about insects. Then answer the questions.

Flying Creatures

by Sienna Jackson

A lot of people do not like bugs and flies. Some people are even afraid of bugs and flies because some can bite or sting. But these tiny living things are interesting creatures.

Bugs and flies are insects. Insects are wild animals. You can't really train insects. But you can learn a lot by watching them. What are you waiting for? Take a look!

All insects have six legs. Many insects also have wings. Butterflies are insects. Butterflies have pretty wings. That is why some people who don't like most insects still like them. If you get a chance, look at these wings closely. But don't touch the wings because this can hurt or kill the insect.

According to the article, why are some people afraid of bugs and flies?

A They are interesting creatures.

B Some can bite or sting.

C They are wild animals.

D You can't train them.

The question tells an effect and asks you to find the cause in the text. First, find the information from the question in the text. Then look for a clue word. The clue word *because* points out the cause. Choice B is correct.

According to the article, why do some people who don't like most insects still like butterflies?

A because butterflies have pretty wings

B because you can train butterflies

C because butterflies are insects

D because butterflies have legs

Look in the text for clues. The phrase *That is why* signals the effect that is in the question. You are looking for the cause. The cause is in the sentence right before the clue words. Choice A is the correct answer.

Why shouldn't you touch a butterfly's wings?

_____

_____

Look at the cause and effect at the end of the article. Here is a sample answer:

You shouldn't touch a butterfly's wings because that can hurt or kill the insect.

Read this article about a city in Texas. Then answer the questions.

San Antonio

by David McKey

San Antonio is a very big city. More than a million people live there. But it was a small town in the 1850s. Fewer than 4,000 people lived there at the time.

Back then, ranch workers herded cattle on the open ranges. They drove the herds to Kansas. It was a long trip and hard work. The men stopped at different places on the trails. San Antonio was one of the stops. That's why San Antonio became an important place in the 1860s.

The ranchers and workers wanted and needed many things. So, many new businesses started in San Antonio. They sold things that the men needed. They traded in leather goods. Many businesses did well.

The railroad came to San Antonio in 1877. As a result, trains could move the cattle to many places. This was faster than a cattle drive. It was also faster and easier for people to get to and from San Antonio. More and more people came to live there. People needed goods and services, so many new businesses started. By 1880, more than 20,000 people were living in the city.

San Antonio became an important place in the 1860s because

A it was a stop on cattle drives   C the railroad had come

B it was a nice place to live   D it had a seaport

The question tells an effect and asks you to find the cause. At the end of paragraph 2, you see the clue words *That's why.* The sentence before that says San Antonio was one of the stops on the cattle trails, so choice A is correct.

What did NOT happen in San Antonio as a result of the railroad?

A More people came to the area.

B People could travel faster and more easily.

C People began moving away from San Antonio.

D Ranchers could move their cattle to many places.

The question tells you a cause (the railroad) and asks you to identify the answer choice that was not an effect. An increase in population, moving cattle to many places, and traveling faster and more easily all happened as a result of the railroad. People did not move away from San Antonio, so choice C is the correct answer.

Making a chart like this one can help you see causes and effects.

Cause	Effect
San Antonio was a stop on cattle drives.	It became an important place in the 1860s.
Ranch workers needed and wanted things.	Many new businesses started in San Antonio.
The railroad came to San Antonio in 1877.	More people came to the area. Ranchers could move their cattle to many places. People could travel faster and easier.

Test Yourself

Read this article about dinosaurs. Then answer the questions.

What Happened to Dinosaurs?

by Maria Santos

People love dinosaurs. They are the best known of all ancient animals. There are books about them. There are movies about them. Children play with toy dinosaurs. Some people wish they could see a live dinosaur. But that's impossible because dinosaurs died out a long time ago, before people walked on Earth.

People have different ideas about why dinosaurs died. Some think a big rock from space hit Earth. As a result, the weather changed. Plants did not get enough sunlight and died. Dinosaurs did not have the food they needed to survive and they died, too.

Others think Earth became too dry and too cold. Dinosaurs did not have enough water to drink because there was less rain. They could not live in such cold. And some people do not believe that dinosaurs died out at all. So where are all these dinosaurs today? They may be birds! Scientists study birds to find out if they are dinosaurs with short tails and feathers.

1 According to the article, why is it impossible for people to see a live dinosaur?

    A because dinosaurs died out a long time ago

    B because there are movies about dinosaurs

    C because there are books about dinosaurs

    D because dinosaurs are toys for children

2 According to the article, what caused Earth's weather to change?

    A people's ideas

    B dinosaurs died

    C a big rock from space hit Earth

    D plants did not get enough sunlight

3 According to the article, what happened to dinosaurs as a result of less rain?

    A They did not have enough water to drink.

    B They could not live in such cold.

    C They turned into birds.

    D They did not die.

4 Explain what could happen if a big rock from space hit Earth today. Use details from the article to support your answer.

_____

_____

_____

_____

_____

_____

Fact and Opinion

Standard 3.2.8

When you read for information, you get a lot of facts. But some of the statements you read may be the author's opinions. An **opinion** tells you how someone thinks and feels. A **fact** can be proven true or false.

So, how can you tell the difference between a fact and an opinion? Look for "opinion word" clues like these:

Guided Practice

Read this article. Then answer the questions.

The Ladybug

by Tyra Carpenter

Ladybugs are everywhere. Chances are you have seen one. Common ladybugs are yellow, orange, or red with small black spots. There are more than 5,000 kinds of ladybugs around the world. Ladybugs are small beetles. They eat tiny insects. Farmers use ladybugs to control pests that feed on their plants.

The correct name for ladybugs is lady beetles. In some other countries, they are called ladybirds. No matter what they are called, ladybugs are a popular insect. There are books about ladybugs. There are songs about ladybugs. It seems like most people don't like to touch bugs. I think these same people will let a ladybug walk on their hand. Everybody loves ladybugs!

Around the world, people believe that ladybugs bring good luck. This idea may have started because ladybugs can save food crops. Or maybe just seeing a colorful ladybug can cheer you up.

Which of these sentences is an OPINION?

A The ladybug has small black spots.

B There are books about ladybugs.

C Ladybugs are small beetles.

D Everybody loves ladybugs!

Remember, a fact can be proven true or false. Choices A, B, and C are statements of fact. You can look up this information to find out if it is true or false. Choice D makes a statement about something that cannot be proven true or false. So, choice D is the answer you want.

Which of these sentences is a FACT?

A I think these same people will let a ladybug walk on their hand.

B There are more than 5,000 kinds of ladybugs around the world.

C It seems like most people don't like to touch bugs.

D These little creatures are everywhere.

"It seems" in choice C and "I think" in choice A show that both these choices are personal opinions. Choice D also cannot be proven true or false. Choice B tells you something that you can look up to find out if it is true or false. Choice B is a statement of fact, so it is the correct answer.

Write ONE FACT and ONE OPINION about your favorite animal.

Fact: _____

_____

Opinion: _____

_____

Think about one thing you can prove and one thing that is a feeling or opinion you have. Here is a sample answer:

Fact: The grizzly bear has larger claws than the black bear.

Opinion: Grizzly bears are the toughest animals in the wild.

Now read a letter to the editor of a newspaper. Then answer the questions that follow.

Dear Editor:

The Daily News printed a letter from Ann Lee on April 21. Ms. Lee's letter was on the Opinion Page. My teacher read the letter to the class. In the letter, Ms. Lee said that kids should not get allowances because they can't manage money. Ms. Lee's ideas about kids and allowances are wrong.

My class took part in a survey last week. The survey was about allowances. There are 28 students in my class. Twelve students get an allowance of $4.00 every week. Ten students get no allowance at all. They get money when their parents agree that they need it. That does not always work. Parents and kids do not always agree on what they need. Six students save money from their birthdays and holidays. That is all the spending money they have.

Most kids would not agree with Ms. Lee. It is only fair that all kids get an allowance. I think we kids can manage our own money. All we need is the chance to learn how. Managing money wisely only comes with practice. Everyone knows that. There is nothing wrong with learning and practicing while we're kids.

All parents should get together. They should talk about giving us allowances. To be fair, they should all decide to do the same thing. They should also teach us how to manage money.

Sincerely,

Kelly Kavanaugh

Which of these sentences is NOT a fact?

   A *The Daily News* printed a letter from Ann Lee on April 21.

   B My teacher read the letter to the class.

   C Ms. Lee's ideas about kids and allowances are wrong.

   D Ms. Lee's letter was on the Opinion Page.

> Choice C is correct. All the other sentences are facts that can be proven. The writer cannot prove that Ms. Lee's ideas are wrong.

In which of these sentences does the writer give an OPINION?

   A My class took part in a survey last week.

   B The survey was about allowances.

   C There are 28 students in my class.

   D Most kids would not agree with Ms. Lee.

> You could prove choices A, B, and C by checking with Kelly's teacher. Choice D is the correct answer. It is the only choice that is an opinion.

In which sentence is Kelly Kavanaugh giving an OPINION?

   A I think we kids can manage our own money.

   B Twelve students get an allowance of $4.00 every week.

   C Ten students get no allowance at all.

   D Six students save money from their birthdays and holidays.

> In choice A, Kelly is speaking for all kids. *Think* is the clue word. There is no way to prove that all kids can manage their own money, so A is correct.

Test Yourself

Read the passage "Why Do Wolves Howl?" Then answer the questions that follow.

Why Do Wolves Howl?

by Jeffrey Caulder

Have you ever heard a wolf howling at night? It can be an eerie, lonely sound. Wolves make a variety of sounds. They bark, woof, whimper, yelp, whine, growl, and moan a lot more often than they howl. But howling defines the wolf. Each wolf has a different howl. No dog howls like a wolf. It's a sad sound. It's a wild sound. So, why do wolves howl?

The center of a wolf's life is its pack. Some people think that howling makes the bond between wolves in the pack stronger. By the time a wolf pup is 6 months old, it has learned the voices of its pack mates. An interesting howl is called the "chorus" howl. A pair of wolves howling together can sound like four or more wolves. Even so, a chorus of howls can end with a fight between pack mates. Some wolves may even be punished for joining in.

We do know that howling keeps a pack together as a group. Wolves wander over large areas to find food. So they are often separated from one another. Of all their calls, howling is the only one that works over great distances. If you separate a wolf from its pack, very soon it will begin howling over and over again.

There are two main reasons that wolves howl. They howl to keep the pack together and to keep enemies away. The enemies are usually other wolf packs. Smaller packs tend to stay quieter, while larger packs howl more often.

Lastly, have you ever heard that wolves howl at the moon? This seems to be a popular idea. But there is no proof of this. Wolves may be more active on moonlit nights because moonlight helps them see better.

1 Which of these sentences is a FACT?

    A A wolf's howl is a sad sound.

    B A wolf's howl is a wild sound.

    C A wolf's howl is a eerie, lonely sound.

    D Each wolf has a different howl.

2 Which of these sentences is an OPINION?

    A Howling is a scary sound.

    B Wolves wander over large areas to find food.

    C Wolves howl to keep their enemies away.

    D Wolves howl to keep the pack together.

3 Read this sentence from the article.

    An interesting howl is called the "chorus" howl.

Is this a fact or the author's opinion? Explain why.

_____

_____

_____

_____

_____

_____

Unit 3
Reading for Literary Response

What is literature? In your reading at school and on tests, it is usually fiction stories. Some stories are realistic fiction; they are like real life. Fairy tales and fables are literature. So are poems and plays. To talk about literature—and to answer test questions—you need to know some special vocabulary. In this unit, you will learn the important terms that people use to talk about literature.

13 Genre and Theme   Genres are different types of writing. Every story you read belongs to a genre. This lesson will help you see what makes each type of literature unique.

14 Story Elements and Structure All stories have characters, setting, plot, and point of view. In this lesson, you will learn how to recognize these story elements. You will also learn about story structure, which is how stories are put together.

15 Analyzing Character   You analyze a character by what the author tells you. The more you know about why characters think, feel, speak, and act the way they do,

the better you can understand and enjoy the story. In this lesson, you will learn to analyze a character.

16 Author's Purpose   Authors write for different reasons. An author might write a funny story to entertain readers, or a nonfiction article about plants to help readers learn more about nature. This lesson will help you recognize the author's purpose—or reason—for writing.

17 Compare and Contrast   This lesson will help you figure out how things you read about are alike (comparison) and different (contrast).

18 Figurative Language   In this lesson, you will learn special ways authors use words to add life to their writing and help readers picture or feel what is happening.

19 Poetry and Plays   Poems and plays look different than other kinds of literature. They are put together in very specific ways. This lesson will show you what to look for in poems and plays.

There are different types, or genres (ZHAHN•ruhz), of literature. Knowing which genre you are reading helps you understand many things about the story. Some genres can be **fiction,** which means that the people and events are made up by the author. Some genres can be **nonfiction,** which means that they are about real people and real events. Every genre is written for a different purpose.

Biographies are an example of nonfiction. Biographies tell about real people's lives. This means that all people in a biography are real and the events are real.

How-to passages are another example of nonfiction. How-to passages give the readers instructions about how to do something. A recipe, a car manual, or the rules of a game all belong to this genre.

Stories are the genre that you read most often. You probably don't need to read very far to tell whether a story is **realistic fiction** (a made-up story that could happen in real life) or a **traditional story.** Traditional stories are passed down from one generation to the next, growing and changing with each retelling, until someone writes them down. They often teach a lesson or try to explain why things happen or are the way they are. Here are four genres of traditional stories:

Fables are short stories that often have animal characters who talk and act like people. Their theme, or main idea, is usually a lesson about the way people behave. A man named Aesop is believed to have written or told many fables, such as "The Crow and the Pitcher."

Fairy tales, such as "Cinderella" and "Rapunzel," have a main theme or lesson. They have a quality of magic about them and often include imaginary characters like giants, witches, and elves.

Legends are stories about the past that may bend the truth a little about real people and real events. They are connected to a particular time and place in history. A hero is usually the main character.

Tall tales may have characters who are real people in history, but the story is fiction. The hero is usually from America's past. Tall tales wildly exaggerate the skills or strengths of these legendary figures like Paul Bunyan, a giant lumberjack. They also try to explain how something in nature, like a mountain, came to be, usually as the result of a hero's work.

A **poem** may tell a story, too, but it is written in verse and the author pays special attention to sound. The lines are shorter, and they are about the same length.

Plays are another example of fiction. Plays are performed by actors on a stage. A play is divided into acts, as a book is divided into chapters. The group of characters in a play is called the cast.

A story, a poem, or a play usually has a **theme.** The theme is the topic or main idea. It is not the same as the plot, which tells what happens. For example, the plot of the "Ant and the Grasshopper" is "An ant saves food for winter, but a grasshopper does not and so it goes hungry." But the theme is "It is wise to plan for the future." Other kinds of literature, such as a realistic story, a poem, or a play may have the same theme.

Guided Practice

Read this story. Then answer the questions.

The Crow and the Pitcher

The weather was very hot and dry. Crow needed a drink of water. He saw a tall pitcher, so he flew to it, hoping to find water inside. But there was only a little bit of water at the bottom of the pitcher. Crow tried to reach it, but he couldn't. He was almost ready to give up, but he really wanted a drink of water. All of a sudden, he said out loud, "I have an idea!"

Crow gathered as many small stones as he could find. One by one, he dropped them into the pitcher. The stones filled up the bottom so the water rose higher. At last, Crow could reach the water. He took a long drink.

"I feel much better now," said Crow. "That drink of water saved my life."

This kind of story is MOST like

A realistic fiction

B a fairy tale

C a tall tale

D a fable

This story could almost be realistic fiction because a real crow might be able to do something like the crow in the story. But notice that the crow in the story is thinking and talking as a person would. Remember that fables are stories with animal characters that talk and act like people. Choice D is the correct answer.

Which sentence BEST states the theme of the story?

A Crows are smart birds.

B All animals need water to drink.

C When there's a will, there's a way.

D A big pitcher can hold a lot of water.

Remember that choices A, B, and D may be true, but they do not state the theme or lesson. Choice C is the correct answer.

What are TWO things you could change in this story to make it fit a different genre? Explain how the changes make the story fit the new genre.

_____

_____

_____

_____

_____

_____

Think about the other kinds of stories you learned about on pages 112 and 113. Here is a sample answer:

I can make this story a fairy tale by taking out how the crow gets the water by himself and adding a fairy godmother who helps the crow get a drink using her magic wand. Now the story has an imaginary character and magic, like other fairy tales.

George and the Cherry Tree

by Edward Davies

George Washington was the first president of the United States. When he was 6 years old, he got a very special gift. It was a new hatchet. George loved the little ax and wanted to use it. He chopped a few sticks in the garden, but that wasn't much fun. Then he tested the sharp blade against the bark of a small cherry tree. Some of the bark chipped away. George did not mean to hurt the tree, but without its bark the tree died.

Later, his father saw what had happened to his favorite tree. He was very angry. He asked George if he knew who had killed the tree.

"I cannot tell a lie," said young George. "I did cut it with my little hatchet."

George's father was so proud that his son had told the truth he did not punish the boy.

This kind of story is MOST like a

A fairy tale

B tall tale

C legend

D fable

You can tell right away that this is not a fairy tale, because there are no imaginary characters or magic. It is not a fable because there are no animals that talk and act like people. Young George is the hero of the story but his strength and skill are not exaggerated, so this is not a tall tale. This is a legend. It is about real people, but the truth of the events is uncertain. Choice C is the correct answer.

Which of these characters would you NOT expect to meet
in this story?

    A another boy George's age

    B George's mother

    C a gardener

    D a princess

> This story is about young George, so you might expect to meet his mother or another boy his age. Some of the action takes place in a garden, so you might expect a gardener to be there. But a princess would be out of place in this story. Choice D is the correct answer.

Which part of this story do you know is true? Which part
might be made up? Use details from the story to support
your answer.

_____

_____

_____

_____

_____

> Think about what you knew about George Washington before you read this story. Here is a sample answer:

> There really was a man named George Washington, who was the first president of the United States. But he might not have killed a cherry tree or said those exact words.

Test Yourself

Read this story. Then answer questions that follow.

Bear and Chipmunk

an American Indian story

Long ago, when animals could talk, a bear was singing to himself as he turned over big logs with his paws to look for food to eat. He sang, "I'm the biggest. I'm the strongest. I can do anything!"

"Is that so?" said a small voice. "Can you really do anything?"

Bear looked down and saw a little brown chipmunk. "Of course," said Bear. "I am the biggest, strongest animal in the woods." He reached out one huge paw and rolled over a big log. "Look at how easily I can do this. I can do anything."

"Can you stop the sun from rising in the morning?" said the chipmunk.

"I never tried to do anything like that," said Bear. He thought for a moment. "Yes, I can stop the sun from rising. I am sure. I can do anything!"

"You are sure?" said Chipmunk.

"I said I was sure," said Bear. He was beginning to lose his temper with the annoying little chipmunk. "Tomorrow morning the sun will not rise. I will stop it!" Bear sat down facing the east. Behind him the sun set for the night.

Chipmunk went into his hole. He curled up in his snug little nest, chuckling about how foolish Bear was.

Bear sat like that all night. Finally, the birds began singing their morning song, and the east glowed with the light that comes before the sun. "Stop!" yelled the Bear. But the sun rose just as it always did.

Bear was very upset, but Chipmunk was delighted. He was so amused that he came out of his hole, singing, "The sun came up. The sun came up. Bear could not stop the sun from coming up."

Bear sat there looking very unhappy while Chipmunk ran around and around, singing and laughing until he was so weak that he rolled over on his back. Then, quicker than a bolt of lightning, Bear shot out one big paw and pinned Chipmunk to the ground.

"Perhaps I cannot stop the sun from rising," said Bear, "but you will not live to see the sunset."

"Oh, Bear," said Chipmunk. "I was only joking. You are the strongest. You are the quickest. You are the best of all the animals." But Bear did not move his paw.

"Oh, Bear," Chipmunk said, "if you would just lift your paw a little, just a little bit, then I could breathe."

Bear lifted his paw just a little bit. Chipmunk squirmed free. Bear swung his paw at the little chipmunk as he ran for his hole. He was not quick enough to catch him, but the tips of his long claws scraped along Chipmunk's back.

Now, all chipmunks have three pale scars on their back as a reminder of what happens when one animal teases another.

1 You would MOST LIKELY find this story in a book of

A plays

B poetry

C realistic fiction

D traditional stories

2 Which part of this story could really happen?

   A A chipmunk sang, "The sun came up!"

   B A bear rolled over a log with its paw.

   C A bear can stop the sun from rising.

   D A chipmunk talked to a bear.

3 Which part of this story could NOT really happen?

   A A bear yelled, "Stop!"

   B A chipmunk curled up in its nest.

   C A chipmunk ran around in circles.

   D A bear pinned a chipmunk to the ground.

4 In a story like this, you would MOST LIKELY meet

   A a dragon

   B flying fairies

   C a talking robot

   D another talking animal

5 What is the theme or lesson of this story? Do you think it is a good lesson? Explain why or why not.

_____

_____

_____

_____

_____

_____

Imagine that you want to tell a friend about a story you just read. Where will you begin? Will you tell about your favorite **character?** Maybe you want to explain the **plot.** That's what happens in the story. Or you could start with the **setting.** That's where and when the story takes place. All these **story elements** work together to make what you read interesting and fun.

An author usually describes how **characters** look and talk. The "talk" part is called **dialogue.** The way a character talks can be as important as what he or she says. Different genres have different kinds of characters. The characters in realistic fiction are usually people. But the characters in a fable might be animals that talk and act like people.

Every story is told from a **point of view.** A story can be told from a narrator's point of view. In this point of view, you'll see the words *he, she,* and *they.* Or, the story can describe events from a character's point of view, sometimes using *I* and *we.* This is called first-person point of view.

The **setting** is where and when a story happens. A story may be set in the past, present, or future, during a certain year, time, or season. Some stories are set in real places. Some are set in a make-believe world.

The **plot** means the events or action of the story. It usually includes a **conflict,** or problem, which is solved (or settled) by the end of the story. Sometimes the conflict is between characters. Or, it can involve two ideas, such as a character's conflict about doing what is right or wrong.

The plot of every story has a beginning, middle, and end. You can understand a story better when you recognize this **story structure.**

- In the **beginning** of a story, you meet the main characters and find out what the conflict is going to be about.

- The **middle** of the story has most of the action. It leads up to the high point, or **climax,** of the story.

- The **end** of the story starts with the climax. This is where you find out how the conflict turns out. You know by then if the story will have a happy ending or a sad one.

Graphic organizers can help you record details and events in a story. A **sequence chart** tells the events in the order they happened. Using graphic organizers helps you to organize your thoughts about story structure in a simple way.

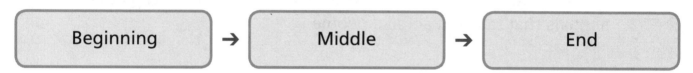

Guided Practice

Read this story. Then answer the questions.

Disaster Area

by Sam Albee

Luis could not find his socks. He could not find his sneakers. His room was a mess, but there was no time to clean it. He had a soccer game in an hour. Only where were his shin guards?

Luis looked under the bed. He pushed aside a few T-shirts, and reached in as far as he could. Then he crawled all the way under the bed, looking for the missing shin guards.

"Luis! Where are you?" his mother called from the doorway to his room.

"I'm under the bed," he said. Then he crawled out, holding his shin guards.

"How can you find anything in this room?" asked his mother. But she didn't wait for an answer. "Come on, I'll help you clean it. We have some time before your soccer game."

Luis gathered all the dirty clothes and put them in the laundry basket. His mother stripped the sheets off the bed. "Look what I found," she said, holding up his special soccer socks. "They were inside the pillowcase!"

Luis put his books on the bookshelf. He threw away some pieces of paper that littered the floor. He put the blocks back in their box. Soon, Luis's room looked much better. "Thanks, Mom," said Luis.

"You did most of it yourself," she said. "Now, let's go play soccer!"

What is the setting of this story?

A Luis's room

B a soccer field

C under the bed

D inside the pillowcase

The setting is where a story happens. The events in this story all take place in Luis's room. Choice A is the correct answer.

From whose point of view is the story being told? Explain your answer using examples from the story.

_____

_____

_____

_____

_____

_____

Think about the words that are used to describe the characters. Here is a sample answer:

The story has the words he, she, and they. This tells me
that the story is being told from a narrator's point of view.

Write what happens at the beginning, middle, and end of the story "Disaster Area."

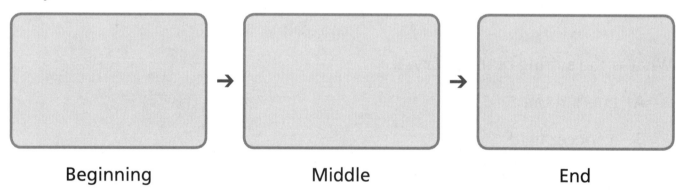

Beginning → Middle → End

Think about the conflict and when you know how the conflict turns out. Here are sample entries:

Beginning: Luis cannot find his soccer things in his messy room.
Middle: His mother helps him tidy up.
End: They find his soccer things and go to the game.

Unit 3 Reading for Literary Response

Read the selection. Then answer the questions.

How Turtle Got Its Shell

a story from Greece

Zeus was the ruler of all the Greek gods. He was powerful, and everyone respected him. The one problem that he had was his bad temper. He was always flinging around thunderbolts. Because of this, many of the other gods were afraid of Zeus.

For his wedding, Zeus invited all the animals to a huge feast. All the animals had a wonderful time. They ate as much as they could and enjoyed all the finest foods. Zeus was happy that everyone had come to his wedding. But as he looked around the party, he did not see the turtle.

"Where is the turtle?" Zeus asked his new wife, Hera. But Hera did not know. Zeus decided to pay the turtle a visit the very next day.

Zeus went to the muddy bank of the river where the turtle lived. When he saw the turtle, he spoke kindly to her. "Turtle," Zeus said. "Why were you not at my wedding feast?"

Turtle tried to hide from the powerful god. This angered Zeus.

Zeus spoke louder this time. "Why were you not at my wedding feast?"

Turtle raised her head nervously. In a tiny, scared voice she said, "There is no place like home."

Zeus began shouting at the turtle, "In that case, you will always carry your home with you wherever you may go." As he spoke, lightning and thunder crashed from the skies. The birds nearby were so scared that they flew into the forest shaking and shrieking with fear.

Turtle suddenly felt a huge weight on her back. It was a hard, heavy shell. Only her little head peeped out, along with her legs and tail to help her move. From then on, turtles have always carried their homes on their backs.

The climax of the story comes when

    A Zeus has a big feast

    B Turtle misses the feast

    C Zeus talks with Turtle

    D Turtle now has a shell

The story begins with Zeus inviting all the animals to his feast. He realizes Turtle is not among his guests. At the end of the story, Zeus gives Turtle her shell. Choices A, B, and D are incorrect. The climax of the story comes when Zeus talks with Turtle about why she did not come to the feast. The correct choice is C.

Which words BEST describe the character of Zeus?

    A quick to anger

    B happy go lucky

    C mad with jealousy

    D easy to please

Zeus is not happy go lucky or easy to please. In the story he is not mad with jealousy. Choices A, C, and D are incorrect. Zeus becomes angry quickly. Choice A is correct.

Which of these is an example of dialogue spoken by Turtle?

A "Where is the turtle?"

B "There is no place like home."

C "Why were you not at my wedding feast?"

D Turtle suddenly felt a huge weight on her back.

Zeus doesn't see Turtle at his feast and asks his wife, "Where is the turtle?" When Zeus visited Turtle he asked, "Why were you not at my wedding feast?" Choices A and C are examples of dialogue spoken by Zeus. Choice D is not an example of dialogue because it is not something that someone said. It is a statement of fact. Choice B is correct. Turtle told Zeus that she missed the feast because "There is no place like home."

The story is told from

A a first-person point of view

B Zeus's point of view

C Turtle's point of view

D the narrator's point of view

The story uses the pronouns *he* and *she* for Zeus and Turtle. This tells you that the story is being told from the narrator's point of view. Choice D is correct.

Test Yourself

Read this story. Then answer the questions.

City Living

by Oscar Gentry

Julio was sad. His family had just moved from the farm where he had lived since he was born. Now they lived in an apartment in a big, loud, smelly city. At least that was what Julio thought of the city. At the farm, he could go outside and play whenever he wanted. Now he was not allowed to go outside by himself. At the farm, Julio had his own room on the top floor of the big, old farmhouse. Now Julio had to share a much smaller room with his older brother. But the worst part of living in the city was that there were no animals. Julio missed the cows. He missed the ducks and chickens.

"Let's go to the park," said his mother. She put some bread in a bag to take with them.

"Is that our snack?" Julio asked. It didn't look very tasty. Usually his mother made a nicer snack than a few slices of plain bread.

"You'll see," his mother said mysteriously.

The park was not far from their apartment, but Julio had not been there yet. His family had been so busy unpacking and settling into their new home, there was no time left for exploring.

The park was bigger than Julio had expected. He thought they were going to a playground, but his mother had another idea. "Let's walk," she said.

Julio liked the park. The trees were as tall as any on the farm. "Here we are," said his mother as they came to a small lake. They sat on a bench.

"May I have my snack now?" asked Julio. His mother handed him an apple.

"Thanks," said Julio. "But I thought the bread was my snack."

His mother took the bag of bread and crumbled some in her hand. She tossed a few crumbs into the lake. Some ducks swam out from the bushes on the side of the lake. "Actually, the bread is *their* snack," she said. Now Julio understood. His mother knew he missed the farm animals. She had brought him here to show him the ducks.

Julio gave the rest of the bread to the ducks. He felt happy for the first time since he had moved to the city. Now he knew that even in a big city, he could find a quiet place to be with animals. He was excited about the other new things he would discover in his new home.

1 What problem does Julio have at the beginning of the story?

   A His mother is angry with him.

   B The park is not like the farm.

   C He misses farm life with animals.

   D He doesn't like bread.

2 Which is NOT a setting in this story?

   A city

   B park

   C farm

   D apartment

3 Write TWO things that happen in the middle of the story.

   _____

   _____

   _____

   _____

Read this story. Then answer the questions.

Long ago, American Indian people depended on corn for food. They planted corn and harvested it when it was ready. Then they dried the kernels and pounded them into cornmeal. They cooked and ate cornmeal all winter when there was no fresh food. The cornmeal was stored in large baskets outside their homes.

One morning, an old woman went to her basket for some cornmeal to make breakfast. She found the basket tipped over. Cornmeal had spilled out onto the ground. And in the middle of this mess was a huge paw print.

The old woman showed her husband the paw print. "What kind of animal stole our cornmeal?" he asked. It looked like a dog's paw print, but it was much bigger than any dog they had ever seen.

"It must be a spirit dog," said the old woman. Soon all the people in the village gathered together to discuss the problem.

"What should we do?" the old man asked. "If the dog comes back and eats all our cornmeal, we will starve this winter."

"We must scare the dog away," said the old woman.

Later, after the sun had set, the people hid near the basket of cornmeal with their drums and rattles. They waited, and waited, until at last the dog returned. The old woman was right. It was a spirit dog. Its fur glowed with a silvery light.

The dog dipped its enormous head into the basket and began to gobble up the cornmeal. All together the people beat their drums and shook their rattles. The loud noise startled the dog. It lifted its head from the basket and started to run away. Its mouth was still full of cornmeal and some fell to the ground as he ran.

The people chased the dog up a hill. They beat their drums harder and shook their rattles even more until the noise was as loud as thunder. The spirit dog raced to the top of the hill and jumped high into the air. Shining white cornmeal continued to fall from its mouth as its silvery body streaked across the night sky.

The dog was gone, but the band of white light stayed in the night sky. The pieces of cornmeal had become stars. The people called it "the place where the dog ran." We call it the Milky Way.

4 The beginning of the story ends when

   A the dog returns to eat more cornmeal

   B the old woman finds the cornmeal basket tipped over

   C the old man asks, "What kind of animal stole our cornmeal?"

   D the old man says, "If the dog comes back and eats all our cornmeal, we will starve this winter"

5 Which sentence tells the climax of this story?

   A The pieces of cornmeal had become stars.

   B The old woman showed her husband the paw print.

   C All together the people beat their drums and shook their rattles.

   D The spirit dog raced to the top of the hill and jumped high into the air.

6 What is the conflict in this story, and how is it solved? Use details from the story to support your answer.

   _____

   _____

   _____

   _____

Standard 3.3.3

A **character** is a person or animal in a story. Characters can be fictional (made up), or they can be real people. Characters make stories interesting and fun to read. A story may be full of action and excitement, but if you don't care about the characters, you may not care much about the story. If you do care about a character, it is probably because the character seems real to you. Maybe the character reminds you of yourself or someone you know.

You analyze a character by what the author tells you. The author of a story can tell you what characters are like in different ways.

- The author may use words to describe how a character looks: *Tina had brown hair and brown eyes.*

- The author may also use words to describe how a character feels: *Felix was upset and angry.*

- The author may show what characters are like by their actions: *Lisa slammed the door behind her.*

- The author may give characters words to say that tell how they feel and think: *"It's not fair," she complained. "I need a new bike. Mom and Dad just don't understand."*

The more you understand about characters, the better you understand a story. As you read, ask yourself, How does the character talk and act? How does the character handle problems? What do other characters say about the character? Remember that characters change and grow in a story, just like real people.

Guided Practice

Read this story. Then answer the questions.

Catching the Tiger

a Japanese folktale

Once upon a time there lived a boy named Ikkyusan. People who knew him thought that he was very wise.

One day, a man decided that it would be funny to play a trick on Ikkyusan. He wanted to see for himself if the boy was as clever as everyone claimed.

The man showed Ikkyusan a drawing of a tiger. The creature looked amazingly real. Its coat was almost the color of an orange. It was marked with thin black stripes. Its huge paws with razor-sharp claws and its large teeth made it look dangerous. Ikkyusan was thankful that it was just a drawing.

As the man showed the drawing, he smiled slyly at Ikkyusan, and asked, "Would you kindly catch this tiger for me?"

Ikkyusan gave the man an odd look. But then he replied, "I can catch the tiger for you. I will need a rope, though. May I use yours?"

The man went along with the boy, handing him a rope. With that, Ikkyusan stepped in front of the tiger in the drawing. He walked back and forth in front of the tiger, as if daring the animal to attack. Then, Ikkyusan suddenly shouted, "Hurry! Please chase out the tiger!"

Without thinking, the man said, "Don't be ridiculous! How can I chase out a tiger in a drawing?"

Ikkyusan replied, "Well, if you can't chase out the tiger, then how can I catch it for you?"

The man's smile quickly turned to a frown. Unable to think of a reply, he turned and walked away. Ikkyusan went back to what he had been doing before.

Which of these sentences BEST describes Ikkyusan?

A He was not a very friendly boy.

B He was as clever as everyone claimed.

C He was not as clever as everyone claimed.

D He was pleased that he had tricked the man.

> There are no clues in the story to show that the boy was friendly or unfriendly. He did not act pleased at the end of the story. He just went back to what he had been doing before. He may have tricked the man, but he did not gloat. The boy showed that he was clever. Choice B is correct.

When the man "smiled slyly at Ikkyusan," he was being

A delighted

C sneaky

B friendly

D funny

> The man must have known that you cannot chase a tiger out of a drawing. He was trying to play a trick on Ikkyusan to see if he was as wise as people thought. When the man smiled slyly, he was being sneaky. The correct answer is choice C.

How do you think the man felt at the end of the story?
Use details from the story to support your answer.

_____

_____

_____

> How do people usually feel when they try to play a trick on another person and the trick doesn't work? Here is a sample answer:

> The story says the man frowned and walked away. The man probably felt embarrassed because he tried to play a trick on a boy, but the man was the one who looked foolish.

Twins Being Twins

by Samantha Morgan

Sofia and Grace were in the bedroom they shared. Sofia was lying on her sister's bed pretending to read, while Grace was looking through her closet. "Where's my new belt?" she asked. "Did you take it?"

"Why do you always accuse me every time you can't find something?" said Sofia.

"Because you always take my things without asking. Besides, my belt couldn't just walk out of my closet all by itself." Grace kept her side of the room neat. She always made her bed in the morning as soon as she got up. She poked through a pile of clothes on Sofia's unmade bed, and found her belt looped through a pair of her sister's jeans. "See, I'm right again."

"You weren't here when I was getting dressed yesterday, or I would have asked," said Sofia. "What's the big deal, anyway? Now you have it back." Sofia knew it was wrong to take her sister's things without asking. She meant to say that she was sorry, but angry words came out instead. It was just that Grace was so perfect all the time. Sofia was sure that her sister had never told a lie. Even though they were identical twins, they were not the same kind of person at all.

"Well, I forgive you, even though you didn't apologize," said Grace.

"Thanks," said Sofia. She didn't feel angry anymore. "So, may I borrow your new sweater?" she asked sweetly.

Graced smiled as she passed the sweater to her sister.

At the beginning of the story, Sofia is lying on her sister's bed, pretending to read. Which sentence tells what this shows about her?

 A She is sleepy.

 B She thinks her sister is boring.

 C She does not know how to read.

 D She is curious about what her sister is doing.

> There's nothing in the story to show that Sofia is sleepy or thinks her sister is boring. It is possible that Sofia does not know how to read, but it is more likely that she is pretending to read because she is secretly paying attention to what her sister is doing. Choice D is correct.

Which of these sentences BEST describes Grace?

 A She hates her sister.

 B She does not hold a grudge.

 C She thinks only about herself.

 D She wants to make her sister feel bad.

> There are no clues in the story that Grace hates her sister, thinks only about herself, or wants to make Sofia feel bad. Grace is quick to forgive her sister. Choice B is correct.

Test Yourself

Read this story. Then answer the questions.

Raccoon and Coyote

a folktale from Mexico

Raccoon was on her way home one afternoon when Coyote jumped out at her. "What a tasty dinner you will be," said Coyote. He licked his lips.

Raccoon was in trouble. She could not outrun Coyote. She quickly came up with an idea about how to get away from Coyote. "How can you think of food at a time like this," she said. "A terrible storm is coming. It will have hailstones as big as melons. They will crush your head if you do not find a place to hide right away."

Now Coyote was scared. "What shall I do? You must help me!"

"Well, I was going to hide inside that hollow log over there." Raccoon pointed to a fallen tree. "But you go ahead and take that spot. I will rush to find another."

"You are too kind, Raccoon," said Coyote. Then, he jumped inside the dead tree. When Coyote was inside the log and could not see her, Raccoon threw some stones at the log. The stones bounced off the wood with a loud crack. "The storm has started," she yelled as she ran away.

Coyote stayed inside the log till night. He never knew that Raccoon had tricked him.

1 Why does Raccoon tell Coyote a storm is coming?

   A She wants to get home before it rains.

   B She sees dark clouds in the sky.

   C She is trying to warn Coyote.

   D She is trying to trick Coyote.

2 Why does Raccoon throw stones at the log?

    A She is trying to hurt Coyote.

    B She is trying to break open the log.

    C She wants Coyote to come back outside.

    D She wants Coyote to think the storm has started.

3 At the beginning of the story, Coyote wants to

    A eat Raccoon

    B be friends with Raccoon

    C go to a restaurant for a tasty dinner

    D hide from the storm in a hollow log

4 In this story, Raccoon can BEST be described as

    A mean

    B funny

    C clever

    D unhappy

5 How does Coyote feel at the end of the story?

   A cold and wet from the rainstorm

   B lucky to have escaped the storm

   C angry at Raccoon for tricking him

   D scared of the hailstones the size of melons

6 How do you think Coyote would feel if he found out
that Raccoon tricked him? Use details from the story to
support your answer.

_____

_____

_____

_____

_____

_____

Authors have different reasons for writing. When you read, it's important to think about *why* the author is writing. What is the author's **purpose?** Who is the **audience?** (The audience is the person or people the author is writing for.) How is the author presenting the information to this audience? You can find clues in the way the author presents information and the details the author chooses to include. Authors support their purpose for writing with their **point of view**—their thoughts, feelings, and beliefs about a topic.

Something with a lot of details, such as a nature magazine, is usually meant to **describe.**

A story or a poem is usually meant to **entertain** or **amuse.** It's "just for fun."

A poster or ad tries to get you to do something. It contains opinions and is usually meant to **persuade.**

A passage full of facts or directions is usually meant to **explain** or **instruct.**

When you read fiction, you need to know who is telling the story. Is it a main character? Or is it someone else, a narrator? It's also important to understand the **tone** or the mood of a story. The tone or mood is the feeling that the author of the story creates. Is it funny? Is it sad? Is it scary?

When you read nonfiction, such as an announcement or a science article, you must figure out why the author wrote it. How does the author present the information? Does it show the author's thoughts and feelings, or does it just give the facts? Is it funny or serious?

Understanding the author's point of view and tone in a passage helps you better understand what you read.

Guided Practice

Read the story and answer the questions.

My Way

For a long time, my parents wanted me to play some kind of sport. They said that I needed the exercise to make me strong and healthy. So I tried soccer, baseball, and swimming. "I can't get good at anything," I told my dad.

"That's because you are not interested, Malik," he said. "You just have to try harder."

My parents gave me a few more ideas of sports to try. But none of them worked for me. Finally, they just gave up.

Soon after that, I started dancing. My friend Abdul and I saw some guys on TV singing and dancing. We thought it was really cool. They did lots of movements with their feet, arms, and heads. We watched videos of these guys performing. Then we imitated what they did. We got really good. Abdul and I found three more boys who are good dancers. Now we perform. Everyone thinks we are super. My parents were surprised. They had to admit that this kind of dancing gives you lots of exercise.

I'm beginning to notice a lot of kids who are really talented at other things besides sports. One kid I know builds soap box cars. Another can weave, so he makes a lot of things. My cousin Jake likes to fish. Those things might not give you much exercise. But when you do something you like and are good at, it has to be good for your health.

What does the author think every kid should do?

A sing and dance

B some kind of sport

C something they enjoy

D whatever their parents say

The author believes that doing what you like to do is most important. The correct answer is C.

Which sentence BEST describes the author's point of view?

A Everyone likes weaving and fishing.

B You should be in sports for your parents' sake.

C Your health comes first, and then you will have time for fun.

D Doing something you like is good for your health.

The last sentence in the passage is the main clue. Answer D gives the author's point of view.

© The Continental Press, Inc. **DUPLICATING THIS MATERIAL IS ILLEGAL.**

Read the play written by a group of third graders. Then answer the questions.

Trouble on the Playground

[Setting: Playground. Slim is throwing a ball in the air and catching it.]

Cal: Hey kid! Let me see that ball.

Slim: No. I'm practicing throwing and catching.

Cal: You better give it to me. I'm bigger than you. You know what that means.

Slim: No.

Cal: Well, I'll just have to take it then.

(He grabs the ball.)

Slim: Give me that! *(He runs after Cal.)*

Cal: You forgot to say please!

(Cal pushes. Slim falls down. Other kids gather around to see what is happening.)

Ben: *(whispers to Sara)* Cal is such a bully.

Sara: My mom says bullies hurt others because they are lonely and sad inside.

(The kids start shouting.)

Kids: Stop it, Cal. Give Slim that ball.

Cal: *(Scowling and angry as he shouts and walks away.)* Oh, all right. I will, but I don't have to.

Slim: Thanks, guys. I didn't want to lose that ball.

Ben: Sara says that Cal might feel sad inside. Maybe we can help him.

Slim: Let's talk to Mr. Greene about it. Maybe he can show us how to be friends with Cal. When he has some friends, maybe he will not be so mean anymore.

Sara: Good idea. Let's go find Mr. Greene.

The kids wrote this play to

A entertain and make people laugh

B persuade people to write plays

C give information about a meeting

D explain something and solve a problem

The writers were not giving information or trying to make people laugh. Their purpose was not to persuade people to write plays. The purpose of this play is to explain the problem of bullying and show how it can be solved. The correct answer is D.

Which sentence BEST describes the writers' point of view?

A There is always trouble on playgrounds.

B Bullies need help to change.

C Bullies should be kicked out of school.

D A bully will never change.

The kids in the play were talking about what they could do to help the bully (Cal) change. Choice B is the correct answer.

The tone of this play is

A scary

B funny

C serious

D sad

This play is about bullying, a serious problem for some kids. The play's purpose and tone is not to be funny or make people laugh. The tone is not sad or scary, because the kids in the play showed they were not afraid of the bully. The correct choice is C.

Test Yourself

Read this article. Then answer the following questions.

Help for the Land

In the past two years, several families had lived in the little log cabin along the river. Some stayed for two months, some for just a few weeks. None of these families seemed to care about the little house and the land where it stood. They knew they were not going to be there long, so they did not bother to take care of the land.

The Hansens lived next door. They watched as the yard filled up with old tires, garbage, and rusty metal. Plastic bags and old newspapers drifted across the yard and down into the river. By the time the last family moved away, the yard was a disaster.

The Hansen family walked around the yard of the empty little house. Kate, the oldest daughter, had an idea. She thought they should call a meeting. They could get the neighbors to help to clean up the yard. So she made some signs. Her younger brother helped her put up the signs around the neighborhood.

Almost everyone in the neighborhood showed up for the meeting. They came with gloves and big garbage bags. They began to work right away. They finished the following weekend. Everyone was so proud of the work they had done. The yard and the little house looked so nice now. And the river was protected.

Any neighborhood group can do what these people did. It just takes organization and people who are willing to share the work. We all need to do our part to make the environment as safe and clean as possible. Is there something that needs to be cleaned up in your neighborhood?

1 What was the author's MAIN purpose in writing this article?

   A to get people to hold meetings where they can discuss things

   B to show that even young kids can help

   C to persuade people that they can do something about the environment

   D to tell people to fix up a house and sell it

2 Which of these was MOST LIKELY Kate's purpose for making signs?

   A to give information about a meeting

   B to complain about a messy yard

   C to make herself look important

   D to get a chance to draw and print

3 Which sentence BEST describes the author's point of view?

    A Everyone needs to clean his or her own yard.

    B Neighbors should tell each other what to do.

    C People should not move to a different house.

    D Everyone must help take care of the land.

Explain how you decided on your answer.

_____

_____

_____

_____

4 The tone of this article is

    A funny

    B sad

    C serious

    D scary

When you read, you often organize information in your mind. One way to do this is to notice similarities (things that are the same) and differences. When you note how two things, actions, or ideas are alike, you're **comparing.** When you note differences between them, you're **contrasting.** This helps you understand what you are reading. It can also help you organize information you get from more than one place or source.

A Venn diagram is a graphic organizer. Information in a Venn diagram compares and contrasts two things. This Venn diagram compares and contrasts two favorite animals.

Cat	Both	Dog
good night vision can climb trees uses litter box	fur, four legs, and a tail good pet	sharp hearing can't climb trees needs to be walked

The middle of the diagram **compares** cats and dogs. It shows how they are similar. The outer part of each circle shows how a cat and a dog are different. They **contrast** the two animals.

Guided Practice

Read these two stories. Then answer the questions.

Why Bear Has a Short Tail

a Native American story retold by Jessica Whitehorse

When the world was new, all the animals could speak to each other. Every morning Bear walked to the lake. He looked at himself in the still water. He saw his long, bushy tail. It looked great! Then he used his quick paws to catch a fish for breakfast.

As Bear walked away from the lake, he called out to other animals. "Good morning, Mr. Fox. Do you see my long, beautiful tail?"

"Yes, Mr. Bear," Fox would answer, "it is a lovely tail."

This went on day after day with Fox, Squirrel, Rabbit, Deer, Moose, and all the other woodland animals. They grew tired of Bear. He always wanted to talk about his beautiful tail. He had no time for things that interested them.

As time went on, spring turned into summer, and summer turned into fall. Bear noticed the beautiful colors of the trees and a chill in the air. But Bear wore a thick, warm coat. He caught a fish every morning, looked at his tail in the lake, and bragged about it to every animal he met. He was happy until one day…

Winter had come. When Bear went to the lake, things were different. He could not see himself in the water. He tried to reach in for a fish, but the lake had turned to ice.

Just then, Otter walked by with a fish in its mouth. "Mr. Otter," Bear said, "please help me." Bear was so hungry he forgot to brag about his tail. "The lake is hard. I cannot catch fish. What should I do?"

Suddenly Otter had a plan. "Mr. Bear, you must find a hole in the ice. Then let your tail hang through the hole into the water. When a fish bites at your tail, pull him up and catch him. It will hurt just a tiny bit, but you will have food."

Bear did not look happy, so Otter added, "With a beautiful tail like yours, you will catch a huge, wonderful fish." Then Bear was convinced.

He found a hole in the ice and sat there with his tail in the lake. Time went by. It got colder and colder. Then Bear heard laughing. He looked around. All of the animals were hiding in the woods laughing at him.

He tried to stand, but his tail was frozen in the ice. He tried again. He was still stuck. Then he pulled with all his might. He stood up all right, but his tail came off. All that was left was a tiny little nub. Bear was so embarrassed that he went to hide.

From then on, all bears have had short, stubby tails. And when winter comes, they all hide in caves or hollow trees and sleep until spring because they are so embarrassed.

How the Crocodile Got Its Rough Skin

an African fable retold by Nan Greer

Long, long ago, the crocodile had beautiful skin. It was as smooth as silk and as shiny as gold.

The crocodile spent his days in the river. But the river water was dark and muddy. The sun could not shine through it. No one could see the crocodile's skin.

One night, when the crocodile came out of the river, the moon was bright. Then the crocodile saw his reflection in the water.

"Oh," he thought, "I am so beautiful! It is too bad that the other animals can't see me better. I have the most beautiful skin! Maybe I should come out in the daytime so they can admire me."

The next day, the crocodile came up out of the water. Sure enough, all the other animals came to drink in the river. When they saw him, they did indeed think he was beautiful. All the animals admired his smooth, shiny golden skin.

The crocodile liked their praise so much that he decided to come out every day. However, each day fewer and fewer of the other animals came to admire him. The crocodile would stay out in the sun longer each day. He would call out to them, "Brothers," he would say, "come see this beautiful skin." But soon, all the other animals ignored him. His bragging was making them mad.

And each day he stayed in the sun, the crocodile's skin got a little darker and a little bumpier. But he didn't notice the changes. He was too busy bragging about his beautiful skin.

One day, one of the birds who came to drink in the river was fed up. "Oh, Brother Crocodile!" she said. "Can't you see that all these days in the sun have made your skin bumpy and ugly?"

The crocodile looked at himself. It was true! His once smooth, golden skin was now thick and dark and bumpy! He was no longer beautiful! The crocodile felt so silly. He crawled back into the muddy river.

And that is why, from that day to this, crocodiles always keep their bodies hidden. They show only their eyes and noses above the water. They are too ashamed of their bumpy skin to come out of the water for long.

What is the MAIN similarity between these two stories?

A They both tell how an animal got that way.

B They both tell how an animal lost its tail.

C They both tell how an animal's skin became dry and scaly.

D They are both tales from Africa.

These stories are just-so stories. They tell how an animal got that way. The correct choice is A. Only bear lost his tail and only crocodile's skin became dry and scaly. Choices B and C are incorrect. Only one tale is from Africa so choice D is incorrect.

If you were making a Venn diagram to compare and contrast these two stories, which information would you put in the section for BEAR?

_____

_____

_____

_____

Here is a sample answer:

Bear loses his tail
Bear likes looking at himself in water

How are crocodile and bear the same?

_____

_____

_____

_____

_____

Here is a sample answer:

Both Crocodile and Bear think they are special. They want the other animals to admire them. They both do something foolish and lose the thing they think makes them special. Crocodile's skin dries out and Bear loses his tail when it freezes in cold water.

Test Yourself

Read these two stories. Then answer the questions.

Why the Sea Is Salty

a folktale from Karelia

There once lived two brothers. One was poor and very kind, and the other was rich and extremely mean. These brothers lived far away from each other. The rich brother lived well in the big city, while the poor brother lived in a shack in the country. So the brothers did not see each other very much.

One day, though, the poor brother and his wife ran out of food. It was the day before a holiday, and they needed food to prepare a good meal. "Oh, dear," said the poor man's wife. "Why don't you go to the city and ask your brother for help? I am sure he will help us!"

"All right," said the man. "I will ask my brother for help. But he is not very kind. This may come back to haunt me."

The next day, the poor man visited his rich brother's house in the city. Although the rich brother did not want to help, he gave his brother a piece of meat to take to the wood-elf, Hiysi, who lived just outside the city near a bridge. In return for the piece of meat, Hiysi gave the poor brother a millstone.

"What will I do with this millstone?" the poor brother asked the wood-elf.

"Well, this stone is very special," the wood-elf replied. "You see, you wish for whatever you want. The millstone will start grinding, and it will keep grinding until you say 'Enough and have done!'"

"Thank you!" the poor man said. Then he ran back home to his wife. When he got home, she laughed with joy.

"I am so glad you are back!" she said. "Did you get food for us?"

"Well," said the poor man, "let's see!" He took out the millstone and placed it on the kitchen table. His wife was about to ask him what it was, but then the poor man said loudly, "I wish for a delicious feast!" The millstone started grinding, and food began to appear on the table! Meat, vegetables, potatoes, cakes—you name it, and it was there! When the poor man thought there was enough food, he shouted, "Enough and have done!" The millstone stopped immediately.

As time went on, the poor man and his wife wished for more things. They wished for nicer clothes, a bigger home, and a lot of food. One day, the poor man's rich brother came over for a visit. "Hey!" he said. "What is this? Where did you get all these fine things?" The poor brother told his rich brother his story. Of course, the rich brother was jealous. "Let me see that stone," he said. Not knowing that his brother would turn against him, the poor man gave his rich brother the stone.

Immediately, the rich brother ran away! "Hey!" shouted the poor brother. "Come back!" But his brother kept running. Finally, the rich brother reached the sea. He hopped onto a large boat, and he began to show off his new stone. The boat happened to be a fishing boat, and the fishermen were about to salt the fish.

"Hmmm," thought the rich brother. "These men would pay a lot of money for some good salt."

"Grind, millstone!" he said. "Make me a lot of wonderful salt!" The millstone started to make salt appear. But the rich brother did not know how to make it stop! The boat began filling up with salt. "Everybody, swim away!" the rich brother yelled. All the men on the boat, including the rich brother, jumped off and swam to shore. When they got to shore, they saw the boat sink. All the fish got away, and all the salt dumped into the water. And, to this day, the seas are filled with salt.

The Tale of Thunder and Lightning

from Southern Nigeria

A very long time ago, Thunder, a mother sheep, had a son. His name was Lightning, and he had a very bad temper. They lived in a small village. When Lightning got angry, he tore through nearby villages, burning houses and knocking down trees.

When Thunder saw Lightning doing these bad things, she would yell at him. Her voice boomed so loud that it shook houses. People had to hold their ears.

When Lightning would hear his mother boom, he would get even angrier. He would start more fires around town. And his mother would yell even louder.

After a while of this, the people in the village could not take it anymore. They asked their king what could be done. The king told Thunder and Lightning to move far away into the wild woods.

Yet, moving away angered them both. Lightning was angry to be sent away. And his mother was mad at him for not obeying her still. Lightning set fires to farmers' crops just outside the woods. And Thunder seemed to become even louder.

The people in the village again begged the king to do something. The king did! He banished both Lightning and Thunder from the earth. He sent them to both live in the sky. That way, Lightning could not set anything more on fire, and his mother could not be heard yelling at him.

This worked for a while. Yet, the people in the village soon saw that Lightning and Thunder were at it again. They saw streaks of light coming from the sky hitting the earth. Then they heard Thunder's voice booming shortly after.

1 What is the MAIN difference between these two stories?

   A only one is a folktale

   B only one has a character who uses magic

   C only one tells how something came to be

   D only one has a greedy character

2 If you were making a Venn diagram to compare and
   contrast these two stories, which information would
   you put in the section for BOTH?

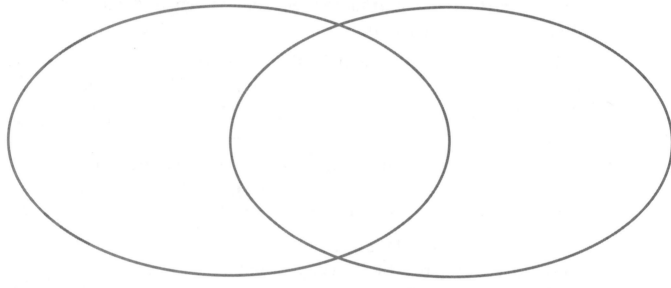

The Tale of Thunder   **Both**   **Why the Sea Is Salty**
and Lightning

Writers use words in different ways to help you picture or feel what is happening. These uses are called figures of speech. Here are some figures of speech that writers use.

An **idiom** is a phrase that has a meaning apart from the words in it. For example, we say that someone "came down with a cold." *Came down with* is an idiom that means "became ill." It has nothing to do with the usual meanings of *came* or *down*.

Another figure of speech is **onomatopoeia** (ah•no•mat•uh•PEE•uh). An onomatopoeia is a word that sounds like what it means. Writers use it to give readers a sense or feeling.

a hissing snake

A **simile** compares two things that are different using the words *like* or *as*. A **metaphor** compares very different things without using the words *like* or *as*: "My sister is a doll."

brave as a lion

Personification is another kind of comparison. The writer makes something that is not human seem like a person in some way.

dancing leaves

Guided Practice

Read this story. Then answer the questions.

A Bad Day Gets Better

by Fran Albert

Pam was feeling blue. She was still in bed after the alarm told her it was time to get up. Her best friend Kim was moving away. Today was Kim's last day at school. The class was having a going away party for her. Pam was bringing cupcakes that she and her mother had baked last night. The cupcakes had pink and white frosting. Pink and white were Kim's favorite colors.

The thought of cupcakes made Pam hungry for breakfast. "I can't stay in bed all day," she told herself as she got up joined her parents in the kitchen. After breakfast, she brushed her teeth and finished getting ready.

"It's raining cats and dogs," said her father as he grabbed his umbrella. Pam put on her raincoat and rain boots. Usually she liked to splash through the puddles. But, today, even that didn't seem like fun.

"I visited my new school," Kim told Pam as they were hanging up their raincoats at school. "The cafeteria lunch tasted like cardboard. I wish I didn't have to go there."

Pam felt like she was going to cry. Kim hadn't left yet, but she missed her already.

That night at dinner, Pam hardly said a word. "You're as quiet as a mouse," said her father. "What's going on?" Pam told her parents how upset she was about Kim moving away.

"We have a surprise for you," said her mother. "I spoke to Kim's parents and we all agreed that you and Kim can go to the same summer camp this year."

"You mean Kim and I will spend all summer together?" Pam said. It sounded too good to be true.

Her parents nodded.

Pam felt as if a weight had been lifted from her mind. Summer was still a long way off, but at least now she had something fun to look forward to.

Which of these phrases from the story has a word that sounds like what it means?

A that night at dinner

B the thought of cupcakes

C splash through the puddles

D sounded too good to be true

The word *splash* sounds like the noise water makes. None of the other answer choices sound like what they mean. Choice C is the correct answer. This is an example of onomatopoeia.

Which of these sentences makes an object seem human?

A We have a surprise for you.

B The alarm told her it was time to get up.

C She had something fun to look forward to.

D The cupcakes had pink and white frosting.

Choices A and C describe humans (the parents and Pam). Choice D describes cupcakes, but doesn't give human qualities. Choice B states that an alarm "told" Pam something. An alarm can't really talk, but a human can! Choice B is the correct answer.

Which sentence compares two things?

A Pam was feeling blue.

B I wish I didn't have to go.

C Pam put on her raincoat and rain boots.

D The cafeteria lunch tasted like cardboard.

> The words *as* and *like* are clues that the author is comparing two things. Choice D includes the clue word *like*. It compares a lunch to cardboard. Choice D is the correct answer.

Which phrase is an idiom?

A as quiet as a mouse   **C** she missed her already

B raining cats and dogs   **D** felt like she was going to cry

> Remember, an idiom is a phrase that has a meaning that is different from the meaning of the words in the phrase. Cats and dogs don't really fall from the sky. Choice B is the correct answer.

Test Yourself

Read the passage. Then answer the questions.

The most unbelievable thing happened to me last night. Mom had said I could read for another 15 or 20 minutes, but then it was lights out. I knew she or dad would check on me, so I pretended to be sleeping. I heard the stairs creak as mom tiptoed down to the living room. Click! *And now for the ten o'clock news….* That was my signal to grab my flashlight and book and pull the covers over my head. I felt like a caterpillar in a cocoon. But I had to find out how the book ended. Would the pioneers be able to cross the mountains before they were trapped by the winter snows?

The last thing I remember was peeking out from under the covers. The clock on my dresser was warning me, "Go to sleep. It's three hours past your bedtime." But I just couldn't stop reading.

When I woke up, I knew that something was wrong. I wasn't in my bed or in my room or in my house. I was on a lumpy straw mattress. The walls were built of logs with clay packed in between. The only window was small and covered with soot. The room was as cold as ice and as smoky as a campfire. It was dark and shadowy like a cave, too. There was just enough light to see two mice running across my quilt.

Mice? I hate mice, so I screamed at the top of my lungs. "Mom! Dad! Where are you? Help me!" Seconds later, it felt like someone was shaking me. Then I heard a familiar voice saying, "Shh. Calm down, Emily. We're right here. Wake up."

When I opened my eyes and looked up, I saw my parents staring down at me. I felt my flashlight and book under the covers. I was back in my house in my room and in my bed. Whew! I must have been dreaming. Thank goodness!

1 What phrase did Emily use to describe how she felt when she was reading in bed?

A pretended to be sleeping

B then it was lights out

C trapped by the winter snows

D like a caterpillar in a cocoon

2 *Click* is used to describe the sound of

   A the flashlight as Emily turns it on

   B the television being turned on

   C Emily's mom tiptoeing down the stairs

   D Emily's clock

3 Which phrase means "very loudly"?

   A a lumpy straw mattress

   B the ten o'clock news

   C at the top of my lungs

   D that was my signal

4 Which of these does NOT help you picture the room in Emily's dream?

   A as cold as ice

   B like someone was shaking me

   C as smoky as a campfire

   D dark and shadowy like a cave

5 Find an object in the story that is described as doing something human. What is it, and what does it do that is like a person?

_____

_____

_____

_____

_____

Poetry

Poetry uses musical language to create word pictures and sound effects in your mind. As you read a poem, here are some important things to think about.

Many poems repeat sounds at the ends of words. This is called **rhyme.** Sometimes the rhyme comes at the end of a line of poetry:

*Twinkle, twinkle little **star,***
*How I wonder what you **are.***

Sometimes the rhyming words appear in the same line:

*Jack and **Jill** went up the **hill***

Most poems have a pattern of stressed and unstressed beats in a line. This is called **rhythm.** A stressed beat has more force than an unstressed beat. Stresses usually come every other beat, beginning with the second beat.

*The **sea** is **calm** to**night***

Sometimes a poem will repeat the same beginning consonant sounds in a line. This is called **alliteration.**

***H**ungry **h**oneybees **h**um as they **h**unt.*

In a **form poem,** or **shape poem,** words are arranged on the page in the shape of a real object, such as a star or a flower. This object is what the poet is writing about in the poem.

Poems are made up of one or more stanzas, or **verses.** The verses of a poem are usually separated by a space between the lines. Look at "Summer Nights" below for an example. You can see that this poem has two verses.

Guided Practice

Read the following poem. Then answer the questions that follow.

Summer Nights

adapted from Mother Goose's
"The Cats Went Out to Serenade"

1   The cats went out to serenade
2   And on a banjo softly played.
3   On summer nights they climbed a tree
4   And sang, "My love, oh, come to me!"

5   They sang so sweetly all the night;
6   And danced under the pale moonlight.
7   The kitties came from near and far
8   To swoon with love under the stars.

In "Summer Nights," which lines rhyme?

A lines 3 and 4

B lines 2 and 3

C lines 4 and 5

D lines 6 and 8

The last words in lines 3 and 4 are *tree* and *me.* They rhyme, as the last words in lines 1 and 2, 5 and 6, and 7 and 8 do. These lines are called *couplets.* Choice A is the correct answer.

Unit 3 Reading for Literary Response

Which of these shows the rhythm of the line with stressed beats in bold?

A **They sang** so sweetly **all the** night;

B They **sang so** sweetly **all** the **night;**

C **They** sang **so** sweet**ly** all **the** night;

D They **sang** so **sweet**ly **all** the **night;**

> Read each line aloud slowly. Listen for where you stress the beats of each line. Stresses usually come every other beat. Choices A and B stress two beats in a row. Choice C stresses every other beat, but it's the wrong beat. Choice D also stresses every other beat. But this time it's the right beat. Choice D is the correct answer.

What beginning sound is repeated most in "Summer Nights"? Give examples of these words and tell which lines or verses they are found in.

_____

_____

_____

_____

_____

Here is a sample answer:

The s sound is repeated most.
It can be found in serenade in line 1,
softly in line 2,
summer in line 3,
sang in line 4,
sang and sweetly in line 5,
swoon and stars in line 8

Read this poem. Then answer the questions.

The Silent Snake

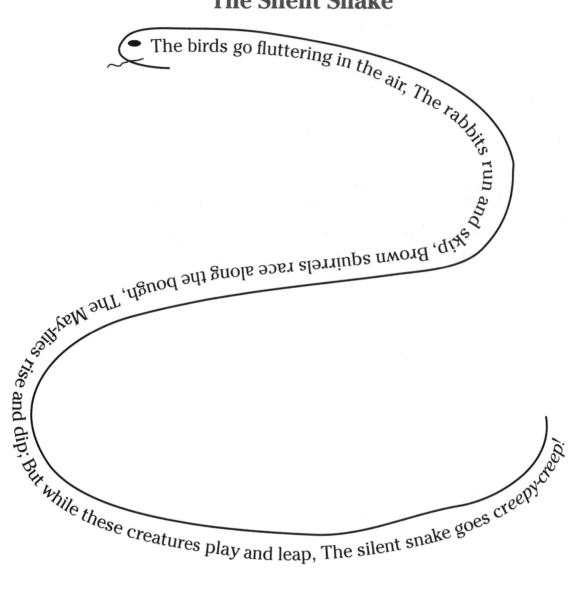

The birds go fluttering in the air, The rabbits run and skip, Brown squirrels race along the bough, The May-flies rise and dip; But while these creatures play and leap, The silent snake goes creepy-creep!

What is the relationship between the shape of the poem and its subject?

_____

_____

Look at the title of the poem and how the poem is printed. Here is a sample answer:

The poem is printed in the shape of a snake, and the poem is about a snake. The poem even has eyes and a tongue!

Unit 3 Reading for Literary Response

Give two examples of **rhyme** from this poem.

_____

_____

_____

Think about what you learned about rhyme on page 163. Here is a sample answer:

There is rhyming with the words <u>skip</u> and <u>dip</u> and with the words <u>leap</u> and <u>creepy-creep</u>.

Test Yourself

Read this poem. Then answer the questions.

The Squirrel

Whisky, frisky,
Hippity hop,
Up he goes
To the treetop!

5 Whirly, twirly
Round and round,
Down he scampers
To the ground.

Furly, curly,
10 What a tail!
Tall as a feather,
Broad as a sail.

Where's his supper?
In the shell,
15 Snappity, crackity,
Out it fell.

1 Which group of words matches the rhythm of line 2 of the poem?

   A Lemon drop

   B Clippity clop

   C Whisky, frisky

   D The treetop

2 Which of these lines from the poem has a repeated beginning sound?

   A Up he goes

   B What a tail!

   C To the treetop!

   D Down he scampers

3 Which lines rhyme in this poem?

   A lines 1 and 3

   B lines 1 and 4

   C lines 2 and 3

   D lines 2 and 4

4 If you wanted to make this poem into a shape poem, which shape would you use? Explain why.

   _____

   _____

   _____

   _____

   _____

Plays

A **play** is a story that is performed by actors on a stage. A play is divided into **acts,** like a book is divided into chapters. Acts may be divided into **scenes.** A scene is part of the action that takes place in one place. When you watch a play or read one, look for these things:

Characters are the people who have parts in a play. A list of these characters is called the **cast.** The cast always appears at the beginning of a printed play or in the program. The name of the actor who plays each part follows the character's name. Sometimes there is a **narrator** who describes events in the play to the audience or reader.

The **setting** is the time and place where the action of the play happens. Sometimes the setting is described in the **introduction** at the beginning of a play. This introduction gives the reader background information about the events and characters.

Stage directions explain how actors should move and speak. In a **script,** or written version of the play, these stage directions are usually printed in *italics* and put inside parentheses, like this: (*laughing*).

Dialogue includes all the words characters speak in a play. In a script, dialogue comes directly after the character's name and any stage directions.

Props are objects, such as books or telephones, that are used onstage by the characters.

Guided Practice

Read act 1 of this play. Then answer the questions.

The Sun and the Wind

based on one of Aesop's fables

Cast of Characters

Sun (a female character)

Wind (a male character)

act 1

Sun and Wind are seated on stools on opposite sides of the stage. They are arguing over who is more powerful.

Wind: I am the most powerful force in the world! I can blow down buildings! I can uproot trees! Nothing on Earth can stand up to me!

Sun: *(rolling her eyes)* Big deal! So you can smash things and make a mess. That's not very nice. I, on the other hand, am a force for good. Look down there. *(She gestures down toward Earth.)* Everything on Earth needs me: plants, animals, people. Nothing could live without me. That's real power.

Wind: *(shaking his head)* So, living things need you. Big deal. That doesn't make you the strongest. We're talking power, not helpfulness.

Sun: *(thinking and tilting her head)* How about a little contest to prove which one of us is stronger?

Wind: Sure! What did you have in mind?

Sun: *(pointing down)* Do you see that man down there—the one walking along the path?

Wind: The one with the long coat?

Sun: Yes, that's the one.

Wind: Well, what about him?

Sun: Let's see which one of us can get that coat off him. Whoever gets the man's coat off is the strongest.

Wind: *(surprised)* Are you kidding? That's just too easy. I know I will win. Just watch me!

Sun: Remember, you can't hurt the man or toss him around. You are just to get the coat off him.

Wind: OK. Here goes.

Wind blows in the direction of the man, while Sun watches.

Sun: *(watching the Wind's effect on the man)* Well, you've got his coat blowing around. But look! He's holding on to it. He's holding it tighter and tighter.

Wind: *(a little out of breath)* I'm just getting started. Just you wait.

Wind blows harder.

Sun: *(shaking her head)* You'll have to blow harder than that. He's hanging on to that coat for dear life.

Wind blows even harder.

Sun: If you keep that up, Wind, you'll blow yourself out. Face it. That man is not going to let you blow his coat off.

Wind, completely out of breath, stops blowing.

Wind: *(trying to catch his breath)* If I can't do it, you surely can't.

Sun: *(smiling)* We'll see.

End of act 1

What is the stage direction in the last line of act 1?

A **Sun:**

B *(smiling)*

C We'll see.

D **Sun:** *(smiling)* We'll see.

> Choice A is the character. Choice C is the dialogue. Choice D is the entire line. Remember that the stage direction appears in italics, inside parentheses. Choice B is correct.

How many characters are there in this play?

A one

B two

C three

D four

> There are two characters in this play: the Sun and the Wind. The man in the coat is not a character, because he never appears on stage and has no lines. So, choice B is the answer you want.

How is this play like a story? How is it different?

_____

_____

_____

_____

_____

_____

> Think back to what you learned about stories earlier in this unit. Here is a sample answer:

> The play is like a story because there are characters, a setting, and a plot. But the play is different than a story because there are stage directions that tell actors how to perform the scene.

Test Yourself

Read act 2 of this play. Then answer the questions.

act 2

Sun and Wind are still seated on stools on opposite sides of the stage. Wind is still breathing hard from his efforts to blow off the man's coat.

Sun: I guess you're not as strong and powerful as you thought you were. You couldn't get the man's coat off.

Wind: *(angry)* If I can't do it, you certainly can't. What are you going to do anyway?

Sun: *(grinning)* I'm going to smile at him. Watch.

Sun looks down at the man and smiles a dazzling smile.

Sun: *(turning to Wind)* See? He's unbuttoning his coat.

Wind: *(muttering)* Big deal. It means nothing.

Sun: He's looking up this way. Now, I'll give him an even bigger smile.

Wind: *(watching Sun and grumbling)* What kind of power is that? You're just smiling at him.

Sun: *(smiling a huge smile)* This is just what it takes. *(She points at the man excitedly.)* Look! He's taking off his coat! I won! I just proved that I, the Sun, am more powerful than you, the Wind.

Wind: *(angry)* It proves nothing of the kind! You didn't take off his coat. He took it off himself.

Sun: We agreed that whoever gets the man's coat off is the strongest. You tried to take it off by force. I made him want to take it off.

Wind: *(sputtering)* Well...it's not fair...you cheated.

Wind gets down from his stool and leaves the stage in a huff. Sun smiles warmly at the audience.

The end

1 Read this line from the play.

> **Wind:** *(angry)* It proves nothing of the kind! You didn't take off his coat. He took it off himself.

What does the stage direction in this line tell the reader?

A how the character Sun feels

B where the character Wind is standing

C the way Sun should say the words

D the way Wind should say the words

2 Which parts of the play appear in **bold?**

A dialogue

B introduction

C stage directions

D names of characters

3 How do you learn about the characters in this play? How is that different from learning about characters in a story? Use details from the play to support your answer.

_____

_____

_____

_____

_____

_____

Unit 3 Reading for Literary Response

Unit 4
Writing on Demand

There are many different kinds of writing. This unit will help you learn to write in different styles. The lessons will also help you improve specific skills, such as planning, revising, and editing.

20 The Writing Process This lesson guides you through the five steps of the writing process. You can use this process on tests and in all the other writing you do.

21 Writing Extended Responses This lesson will guide you through writing an essay as an answer to a test question.

22 Writing Narratives This lesson explains the characteristics of narrative writing. There are tips that guide you through the steps of writing a narrative piece, including planning, writing, and editing.

23 Writing Descriptive Pieces Sometimes you are asked to describe a person, place, thing, or experience. This lesson explains the characteristics of descriptive writing.

24 Writing Persuasive Pieces This lesson explains how to write a piece that persuades someone to take action or to respond. To make your writing stronger, use facts and examples to support your writing. This lesson will show you how.

25 Writing Informational Pieces This lesson discusses the characteristics of informational writing. Skills that will help you include planning, writing, and editing.

26 Writing Responses to Literature When you write about literature, you have to pay attention to all the skills you learned in Unit 3. It also is important to use the writing skills you learned in this unit. This lesson will guide you through writing short responses and extended responses to questions about literature.

The Writing Process

Standards 3.4.2, 3.4.6–8

Writing is a process—something you do in steps. Most writers go through a **writing process** that leads up to publishing their work, so others can read it. You will write better long answers to test questions if you follow these steps:

| Prewriting: Plan your writing. | → | Drafting: Write your answer. | → | Revising: Make your writing stronger. | → | Editing: Get the details right. | → | Publishing: Hand in your test. |

These five steps are useful whether you are writing a story, an essay, or a single paragraph.

Not all writers use the process the same way all the time. Sometimes when you have to write something quickly, like on a language arts test, you won't have the time or space to revise your work. You have to plan as you go along and get the details right the first time. And "publishing" means handing in the test to your teacher.

This lesson will show you how you might use the writing process to answer the sample question below.

Many birds can fly. Some can swim. Write an essay that compares and contrasts two kinds of birds: eagles and penguins.

Be sure to include in your answer:

- how eagles and penguins are similar
- how they are different

Prewriting

- Think about what you know.
- Identify your purpose and audience.
- Think about the points you want to make.
- Plan your writing: make lists, take notes, and make charts.

Drafting

- Have a clear main idea and supporting details.
- Write clearly and briefly.
- Organize your ideas in a way that makes sense.

Revising

- Read over your writing with your purpose and audience in mind.
- Be sure it makes sense. Reorganize as necessary.
- Add facts and details that support your main idea.
- Remove details that are not needed or are repeated.

Editing

- Pay attention to the rules of English, such as capitalization, end marks, and complete sentences.
- Check spelling.

Publishing

- Review your final copy, and then let someone else read it.

Step 1: Prewriting

Prewriting is planning. In this step, you think about what you will write and then organize your ideas. You need to think about:

> - who will read it (your audience)
> - what you will write about (your subject)
> - why you are writing (your purpose)
> - how you will say it (your voice)
> - what you will say (the content)

On a test, some of these things are already decided for you. Your audience is whoever will be scoring the test. The question tells you the subject: eagles and penguins. It also tells you the purpose: to **compare and contrast.** Other questions may have a different purpose. They may ask you to describe, summarize, or explain. Your purpose can help you decide on the "voice" you will use. For example, if you were writing a letter to a friend, your writing would have a friendly tone. In this case, you are writing an essay. So your writing should be more serious.

Now you need to think about the content. Content is the information you present. What will you say that will describe how eagles and penguins are alike and how they are different?

First, make sure you are clear about your main idea. Your main idea should summarize what the question is asking you to do. All the facts, details, and opinions you write should support this main idea. Try to write your main idea in a single sentence:

Eagles and penguins are both birds, but they still have many differences.

Sometimes it helps to use a graphic organizer when you are planning your writing. For this question, you might use a Venn diagram to organize your information.

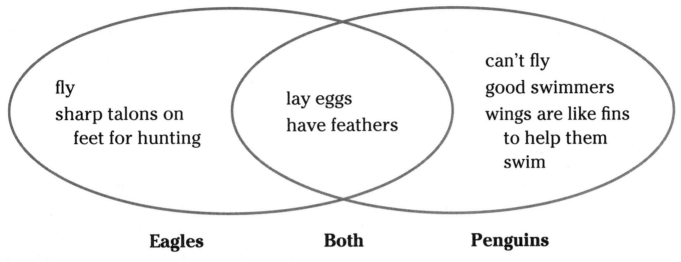

| Eagles | Both | Penguins |

To plan other kinds of writing, you can use other graphic organizers:

An **outline** or **web** can help you identify main ideas and supporting details.

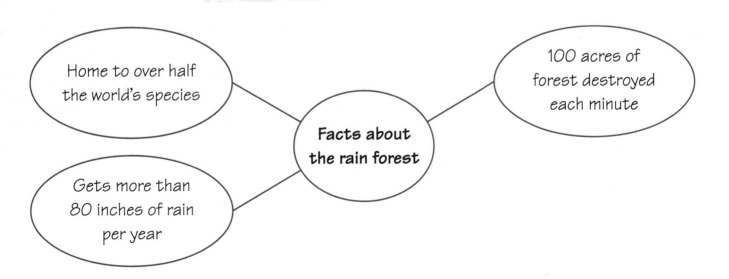

A **sequence chart** is useful when you are writing a story with a beginning, middle, and end. It helps you map out events in the order they happened.

| Diana got up. | → | She ate breakfast. | → | She got dressed. | → | She went to school. |

Step 2: Drafting

After you plan your work, you need to put your main idea and supporting details into sentences and paragraphs. This step is called **drafting.** Drafting is where you do most of the writing. You'll make changes and corrections later. Here is a draft based on the Venn diagram in the prewriting plan.

Eagles and penguins are both birds. Like all birds, both eagles and penguins have feathers and lay eggs. But eagles and penguins are very different kinds of birds. They look different.

Eagles have sharp claws called talons on their feet. This helps them catch small animals to eat. They have big wings. Sometimes you can see eagles flying in the sky.

Penguins cannot fly. There wings look like flippers. This helps them swim. Penguins spend a lot of time in water. They eats fish. I don't like to eat fish. Penguins live where it is very cold. They have a layer of fat called blubber under their skin. blubber helps keep them warm. Eagles do not have blubber.

Step 3: Revising

When you have finished your draft, you need to read it carefully and make changes to improve your writing. This is called **revising.** When you are drafting, you focus on your own ideas and what you know and think about the topic. When you are revising, you think about your audience. Ask yourself if the person reading your work will understand what you are trying to say.

When you revise, you might need to change the content of your work. Or, you might revise the order of things. Asking yourself these questions can help you decide what changes you should make to improve your writing.

- Does my writing have a main idea? Does everything I have included support my main idea and my purpose for writing? Will people understand the point I am trying to make?

- Have I included enough details? Have I included details that are not important? Should I add an important detail or example somewhere?

- Are the relationships between my ideas clear? Do I need to add words, phrases, or sentences to make them clearer?

- Are my sentences well written?

The next example shows how the essay about eagles and penguins could be revised. See if you can figure out why each change was made.

Eagles and penguins are ^(alike in some ways. They are) both birds. Like all birds, both eagles and penguins have feathers and lay eggs. ^(They both make nests.) But eagles and penguins are very different kinds of birds. They look different. ^(Penguins are shaped like a torpedo.)

Eagles have sharp claws called talons on their feet. This helps them catch small animals to eat. They have big wings. Sometimes you can see eagles flying in the sky.

Penguins cannot fly. There wings look like flippers. This helps them swim. Penguins spend a lot of time in water. They eats fish. ~~I don't like to eat fish.~~ Penguins live where it is very cold. They have a layer of fat called blubber under their skin. blubber helps keep them warm. Eagles do not have blubber.

Step 4: Editing

Now you have revised your work and are happy with it, but you're still not done. Revising is for making the big corrections. The next step is **editing**—correcting the little mistakes. When you edit, you make sure that:

- Words are spelled and capitalized correctly
- Punctuation marks are used correctly
- Subjects and verbs agree
- Pronoun forms are right

To edit your essay, go over it sentence by sentence and word by word. Mark the places that need to be corrected. This is called **proofreading.**

When you proofread, you can use some of these marks to show your changes.

Proofreading Symbols		
∧	Add letters or words.	This game is played ^{on}∧ a board.
⊙	Add a period.	It is popular in Japan⊙
≡	Capitalize a letter.	≡two players take turns.
⌃	Add a comma.	You learn about history⌃ culture, and legends.
/	Make a capital letter lowercase.	The R/ules are simple and easy to learn.
ℰ	Take out letters or words.	We have the ~~board and~~ game.

Now look at the corrections you would find when you proofread the essay about eagles and penguins.

Eagles and penguins are alike in some ways. They are both birds.

Like all birds, both eagles and penguins have feathers and lay eggs.

They both make nests. But eagles and penguins are very different

kinds of birds. They look different. Penguins are shaped like a torpedo.

Eagles have sharp claws called talons on their feet. This helps

them catch small animals to eat. They have big wings. Sometimes you

can see eagles flying in the sky.

Penguins cannot fly. ~~There~~ **Their** wings look like flippers. This helps them

swim. Penguins spend a lot of time in water. They ~~eats~~ **eat** fish. Penguins

live where it is very cold. They have a layer of fat called blubber under

their skin. ̲blubber **B** helps keep them warm. Eagles do not have blubber.

Step 5: Publishing

Publishing is making your writing public by sharing it with others. Writers publish their work in books, magazines, and on the Internet. With a test, the publishing step is simple: You just hand in your test paper.

Test Yourself

Use the writing process steps to answer this question. First, read the question carefully. Use the space below for prewriting. Then turn the page to write your draft.

Which kind of trip would you rather take, to the beach or to the mountains? Write an essay that compares and contrasts the two kinds of trips.

In your essay, be sure to explain:

- how the beach and the mountains are alike

- how the beach and mountains are different

- which kind of trip you would rather take

Prewriting

Use an outline or graphic organizer to plan your writing.

Drafting

Now that you have thought about the topic and organized your ideas, write a draft of your essay. Your draft should give the ways the two trips are alike and are different.

_____

_____

_____

_____

_____

_____

_____

_____

_____

Revising, Editing, and Publishing

- Read your draft carefully. Is your main idea clear? Do the facts, details, and opinions support your main idea? Are your sentences well written?

- Check your writing for correct spelling, punctuation, capitalization, and grammar.

- To publish, write your final answer on a separate piece of paper and hand it in.

Some test questions ask you to write an **extended response.** That is an answer longer than one paragraph. You may be asked to explain something about a story or an article. You may be asked to write about a personal experience. When you answer questions like these, you're writing an **essay** and need to use the writing process.

With short answers, you're usually writing only one main idea and supporting details. With an essay, you may need to include several main ideas. The main ideas of all paragraphs become supporting details of the whole essay.

You have to plan an extended response. You have to organize your ideas carefully. On a test, you may get a planning page to do your prewriting. You may have two or more pages for writing your essay. Remember to allow time for revising and editing. Then your writing will be the best it can be.

Not all essays are alike, of course. Usually, your first paragraph will be an **introduction** that states the main idea. It should catch the reader's attention and make her want to read further. The next few paragraphs form the **body** of the essay. Each paragraph has its own main idea that supports the main idea of the essay. The last paragraph is a **conclusion.** It summarizes the ideas in the rest of the essay.

Other things you should do when you're writing an extended response for a test are:

- **Identify what the question asks you to do.**
- **Plan your answer.**
- **Build paragraphs carefully.** The first sentence should clearly state the main idea of your answer. Each sentence that follows should contain details that support the main idea. You may want to write a concluding sentence that connects back to the main idea.

Guided Practice

Read this article. Then answer the question.

Starlings

by Cynthia Sawyer

In 1890, a man brought 100 starlings from Europe to the United States. He let these birds go in New York City's Central Park. Today, there are close to 200 million starlings in the United States.

Some people think a starling is a pretty bird. Its black feathers shine with a purple gloss. They are tipped with cream-colored speckles. But starlings take over the nesting areas of woodpeckers, swallows, and other native birds. Their waste litters the ground and can spread disease. Flocks of starlings near airports can cause airplane accidents. For these reasons and others, many people think these birds are pests.

Starlings will eat almost anything. They eat insects, snails, frogs, worms, berries, and many kinds of fruit. They also eat farmers' crops and the feed farmers put out for their animals. A flock of 1,000 starlings can eat a ton of cattle feed in a month. That's a *small* flock. Sometimes there are so many they look like a black cloud in the sky.

By the 1970s, flocks of 100,000 starlings were not unusual. They were causing huge amounts of damage and loss. People tried many different ways to stop the birds. They trapped and killed them. Farmers poisoned them. They spread nets over their fields. They put plastic over their animals' feed. They brought in falcons hoping that these bigger birds would hunt and kill the starlings. In cities, people cleared away wild plants that bear fruits, nuts, or berries. They scared starlings away with recordings of loud noises.

None of these ideas have solved the starling problem. "Regardless of how we feel about starlings, they are very good at living in the environments we make," explains a bird scientist from New York.

Suppose that some cities in Indiana are having trouble with a kind of ivy. The ivy was brought here from Africa to plant in gardens. Now it has spread out of control. It covers over and kills trees and other plants. Some people want the government to bring in a kind of insect that does not live in Indiana. In Africa, the insect keeps the ivy under control by eating its roots. Write an essay explaining why you think this would be a good idea or a bad idea. Use details from the article about starlings to support your answer.

In your essay, be sure to explain:

- how the starlings in New York got out of control

- your thoughts about bringing a new kind of insect to Indiana

- what other ways might be tried to control the ivy in Indiana

Use the writing process to answer this question. Read the question again carefully. Then do prewriting. The question suggests that your main idea should be:

It would be a good idea to bring in the insect because...

Or:

It would be a bad idea to bring in the insect because...

Note the details in the article about starlings that you can use to support your main idea.

The next step is writing your draft. The first paragraph should state your main idea strongly and clearly in a way that grabs a reader's attention.

The next few paragraphs should support the main idea. You need to explain why it's a good idea or a bad one using information from the article about starlings. Be sure to address the three points in the question. One paragraph might **compare and contrast** information about the starling and the ivy. Another might **draw conclusions** from that information to support your main idea. The next paragraph might **summarize** other ways to control the ivy, using information from the article and question and what you already know.

The last paragraph should bring your essay to a strong conclusion. In it, you might summarize the main ideas of each paragraph and how they support the main idea of your essay.

When you finish writing your draft, revise and edit your essay. Then write your final answer to the question on another sheet of paper. Here is a sample of a final answer.

Some people think we should bring in an African insect to control the spread of African ivy in Indiana. I do not agree with this. Bringing in a bug that doesn't live here naturally is a very bad idea.

The starling is a bird that lived in Europe. A man brought some of these birds to New York City. He let them go in Central Park. He thought that was a good idea. Now there are millions of these birds flying all over America. They are awful pests. They eat farmers' crops and animals' feed. Let's not make this same mistake again. Maybe these insects eat ivy roots in Africa. But how do we know what they will eat here? Maybe they will eat other plants, too. What will we do if this insect eats our food crops? Bring in another animal to eat them? That could go on forever.

There may be other ways to control the African ivy. There are weed killers that work on other pest plants. Maybe animals that already live here, like sheep and goats, will eat the ivy. Or people could dig up the ivy plants.

Bringing African ivy to Indiana was a mistake. Bringing in African insects could be an even bigger one. We should find another way to solve Indiana's ivy problem.

Test Yourself

Read the following article about bears. Then answer the question that follows.

Bears in Pine Canyon

Have you ever seen a bear in the wild? You might have been camping or simply taking a morning walk. It can be an exciting but scary experience. Last summer in Pine Canyon Campground, Corey Stone was hiking with his friends Jen Shaw and Carlos Gomez. As they ate lunch in a clearing off the trail, Jen spotted a black shape moving in the bushes. When Jen pointed to the shape, Carlos knew it was a black bear. He told his friends to get up and leave their food behind. "Back away slowly," he said. "Whatever you do, don't run." The three friends rose to their feet

as the bear came closer. "Can he smell our food?" Jen asked. "Bears have a great sense of smell," Carlos replied. "That's probably why it is here." Corey, Jen, and Carlos backed away slowly, facing the bear. This was the right thing to do. As soon as they got back to camp, they reported the bear to a forest ranger. This helped keep both the hikers and the bear safe. These hikers did the smart thing. *What would you do?*

Many people see bears when they are in the campground. After all, they're in bear country. If you show respect to bears and their home, they will respect you.

Here are some ways to camp safely in bear country:

- When hiking, make noise so you won't surprise a bear. Bears don't want to meet you any more than you want to meet them.
- Avoid berry patches. These are prime feeding areas for bears.

- Watch for bear tracks and be aware of what is around you.
- Report bear sightings. This helps forest rangers keep track of the bears living there.
- Don't litter! Food and trash attract bears. Dispose of all trash in bear-proof containers.
- Most importantly, never feed a bear. This teaches it to relate food to people. It also makes the bear less afraid of people. In the long run, this may result in a problem bear.

If you meet a bear:

- Never run. Running may make a bear chase you.
- Keep your distance. Back away slowly, facing the bear. A bear only attacks if it feels threatened.
- Be extra careful about bear cubs. If you see a cub in the woods, chances are the mother is nearby. Mother bears are very protective of their cubs. Leave the area quickly.

Remember, people create problem bears. The bears are not born that way. We are visiting their home, so we should give them the respect they deserve. That is the only way we can live, camp, and hike in the same places in peace. Bears may look cute and cuddly, but they are not teddy bears. Bears in the wild are just that—wild.

1 Some people want bears removed from the Pine Canyon Campground. They say the bears make the area dangerous for campers. Ms. Chainey is the Director for Wildlife Services in the area. Write her a letter. In your letter, tell why you think the bears should or should not stay in the campground.

In your letter, be sure to explain:

- your personal opinion for or against the bears

- suggestions for how campers and bears can exist together safely or reasons why they cannot

Use the space below to plan what you are going to write. Then write your response on a separate sheet of paper.

Writing Narratives

Standards 3.5.1, 3.5.3, 3.5.4

Have you ever written a story? If you have, then you have written a narrative. A narrative is writing that tells a story. Narratives can be about many different things. You can tell a fictional, or make-believe, story or a story based on real events. You can even write about things that have happened to you in story form.

When you write a story, you need a clear beginning, middle, and end. You write the details in a story in the order that they really happened. If you wrote the end before the middle, readers would be confused. The story would not make sense.

You also need to tell the reader when the story took place. You do this by using details that tell when the action took place. If the story took place a 100 years ago or a 100 years in the future, the setting, details, and descriptions in your story would be different from descriptions and details about what life is like today.

When writing a narrative be sure to:

- tell about the events in the order that they happened

- use details that make the story seem real

- write about the place and the time when the story takes place

When you are asked to write for a test, you are given a writing prompt. A writing prompt is a test question that will tell you what you will write about. Here is an example of a narrative writing prompt:

Think about a special time you had with someone in your family. Write a story that describes that time and explains how you felt that day.

Guided Practice

Read the question and answer below.

Write a story for the first graders in your school about your first day in first grade. Be sure to write details about your school, your teacher, and other students. Write details that tell what you remember from this day. Write the details in the order in which they happened.

Here is what a student named Jenna wrote.

> I remember my first day in first grade. I wore a new blue dress with a cat on the pocket. I was too scared that morning to eat my cereal. My mother waited at the bus stop with me. After I got to school, I got lost in the hallway. A girl in the fifth grade took me to my classroom. Everyone was already there. First, my teacher told my class her name was Mrs. Rosencrantz. She gave us new pencils and a notebook. We wrote some new words. Later we went to the cafeteria to eat lunch. I spilled milk on my dress by accident. We played counting games after recess. Then the bus came to take me home. I loved school but I was very tired. I took a nap when I got home.

What is the first detail Jenna wrote about?

She wrote about what she wore.

What is the last detail Jenna wrote about?

She wrote that she was tired and took a nap when she came home from school.

Test Yourself

Read the article below. Then answer the question.

Local Girl and Her Dog Are Winners

Ariel Gilbert started running in the Henryville 5K Spring Race when she was 10 years old. Now she is 15 years old. Ariel never won the race, but she always felt like a winner. Why? Ariel Gilbert is blind.

Everyone told Ariel she cold not run in a race. But Ariel wanted to run. When she ran, her faithful guide dog led the way. Ariel knew that she could finish a race with the help of her dog Bruno. Luckily, Bruno is quite a runner! Every year both Ariel and her dog have crossed the finish line at Henryville. But Saturday's Henryville 5K Spring Race was different. This time, Ariel was ready to win.

This year, Ariel tried out for her school track team. The coach let Bruno run with Ariel. She ran in cross-country races. Bruno ran with her. They both trained hard. In Saturday's race, her dream came true. Ariel Gilbert was the first blind runner to win the Henryville 5K.

1 Pretend that you were at the Henryville 5K Spring Race. Write a story about Ariel winning the race.

In your story, be sure to:

- write events in the order that they happened

- use details that make the story seem real

- write about the time and the place of the story

Use the space below to plan what you are going to write. Remember to write the details in time order. Next, write your response on a separate sheet of paper.

Writing Descriptive Pieces

Standards 3.5.2, 3.5.3, 3.5.4

Have you ever been asked to use words to create an image about a person, place, or thing? If you have, you have done descriptive writing. When you describe something, you choose the details that give the clearest picture of your subject.

In descriptive writing, you "paint a picture" for a reader by using details that relate to the senses. Maybe you have been asked to write about your grandmother's kitchen. You might use details like the color of the kitchen or the feel of the table.

The topic sentence in a descriptive paragraph introduces the subject. The details that follow help bring it to life. The last sentence sums up the feeling you get about what is being described.

A descriptive writing prompt often asks you to describe a person, place, or thing. You may be asked to describe a favorite teacher, subject, or movie. Below is an example of a descriptive writing prompt.

> Think about one of your favorite vacation spots. Write an essay that describes this place.

Guided Practice

Read the writing prompt. Then answer the question.

> Write a paragraph for your class newsletter about a restaurant you have visited. Use details to describe this place and bring it to life. Talk about what it looks like, sounds like, smells like, and feels like.

The prompt asks you to "use details to describe" so you know you are writing a descriptive piece. You are told to write about a restaurant you have visited so you know you are writing about your own life. You know that you are writing for students your own age because this piece is for your class newsletter.

Here's a student's writing response. This student used a five-senses web to plan her writing.

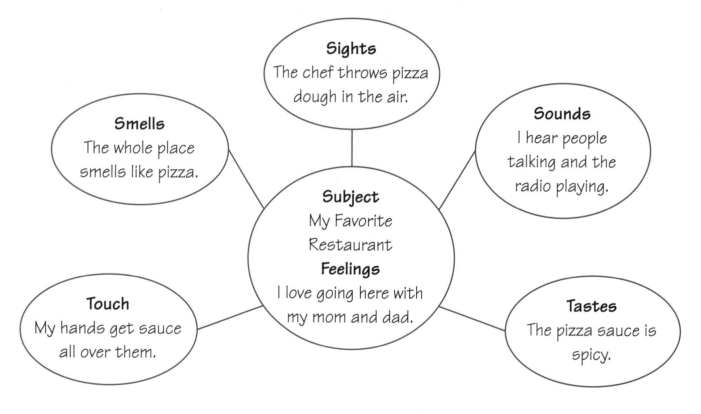

Here is the student's draft. Do the details describe the restaurant well? Do the details support her main idea? Do you get a picture in your mind when you read?

My favorite restaurant is Prato. It's a pizza place the chef throws pizza dough in the air and you can watch him cook. It's loud and you can hear people taking all the time. The radio plays old songs. The whole place smell like pizza it makes me hungry. We get the tomato pizza. I have to be carful not to burn my mouth. The pizza sauce is spicy. The crust is very crunchy I always get my hands messy. I love going here with my mom and dad. we go every friday.

What words did the student use to describe tastes and sounds?

The student uses the words *loud, talking all the time,* and *plays old songs* to describe the sounds she hears.

She uses the words *burn, spicy,* and *crunchy* to describe what she tastes.

Here is the revised draft of the student's piece.

My favorite restaurant is Prato. It's a pizza place ∧ **where** the chef throws pizza dough in the air ∧ and you can watch him cook. It's loud ∧ **in the restaurant** and you can hear people ta∧**l**king all the time. The radio plays old songs. The whole place smell∧**s** like pizza ∧ **and** it makes me hungry. We ∧ **always** get the tomato pizza. I have to be car∧**e**ful not to burn my mouth. The pizza sauce is spicy. The crust is very crunchy ⊙∧ I always get my hands messy. I love going here with my mom and dad. we go every friday. ∧ **I know my friends would love this restaurant, too!**

Test Yourself

Read the writing prompt below. Then plan, write, and proofread your response.

Write a description of your favorite place. Use clear details.

Use the space below to plan what you are going to write. Then write your response on a separate sheet of paper.

Standards 3.5.3, 3.5.4, 3.5.6

Persuading means convincing someone else to take action or respond. When you write to persuade, you need to organize your ideas. Start your persuasive paragraph with a topic sentence that gives your opinion. Your opinion is what you think or feel about a subject. Support your opinion with facts, examples, and reasons to make your point. Remember that facts are statements that can be proved. Your last sentence should be a strong ending that sums up your paragraph.

On a test, a persuasive writing prompt often asks you to persuade someone else to act or respond to what you have written. Below is an example of a persuasive writing prompt.

> Write a persuasive letter to your principal asking him to allow you and a group of friends to have an after-school foreign language club.

Guided Practice

Read the writing prompt. Then answer the question.

> Write a letter to the school board that will be printed in your school newsletter. You want to convince the school board that the new sports field should have a track for runners. Be sure to tell your opinion clearly in the first sentence. Use facts and examples, not opinions, in your supporting sentences.

The prompt asks you to "convince the school board." It also asks you to give your opinion that the new field should have a track. You know that you are being asked to write a persuasive piece. Your audience is both students and adults. You are writing for the adults on the school board and the students who read the school newsletter.

Here's a student's writing response. This student used a chart listing his main opinion and the facts supporting this opinion.

Main Opinion:

> I think that the new sports field should have a track for runners.

Facts:

1. Running is good exercise.

2. Kids who play other sports need to run when they practice.

3. The running track would not take up all the space of the new field. There would be room for other sports.

4. Kids who don't play sports can use the track to get exercise.

Here is the student's draft from his main opinion and fact chart.

March 3, 2009

Dear School Board,

I think that our new sports field should have a running track around it. Running is great exercise. All the gym classes need a place to run. The sport teams need to run when they practice. A running track would go around the playing area so it wouldn't take away from soccer or baseball. Everyone could use it. I love to run. Kids who don't play sports could use the track, too. Everyone wins if we get a new running track!

Sincerely,

Julio Rodriguez

Unit 4 Writing on Demand

What is the topic sentence?

I think that our new sports field should have a running track around it.

What is one fact used to support the student's opinion?

All the gym classes need a place to run.

Test Yourself

Read the writing prompt below. Then plan, write, and proofread your response.

Write a letter to your family persuading them to serve your favorite foods on your birthday.

Use the space below to plan what you are going to write. Then write your response on a separate sheet of paper.

Standards 3.5.4, 3.5.5

When you write a report, you are writing an informational piece. You also use this type of writing to answer a question on a test. Textbooks, cookbooks, and newspaper articles are also examples of informational pieces. Informational writing should give facts, details, and examples. It should be clear and easy to read.

Informational writing needs to be well organized. You can use different methods to organize an informational piece. One way is by main idea and details. Another is by cause and effect. Or you could write the steps for directions in the correct order.

On a test, an informational writing prompt often asks you to think about something in your life and write about it. You may be asked to write about a person you look up to or about a topic, such as animals. Below is an example of an informational writing prompt.

> Think about something you have created. Maybe it's a dessert, a birdhouse, or a skate ramp. Write an informational piece explaining the steps you would take to make your creation.

Guided Practice

Read the writing prompt. Then answer the question.

> Write a paragraph for your classmates explaining how to plant a windowsill garden. Use chronological order to explain the steps you would take.

Here's a student's writing response.

To plant a windowsill garden, you will need a glass container and a lid, gravel, potting soil, small plants, and water. First, place about 2 inches of gravel in the bottom of the glass container. Cover it with about 4 inches of potting soil. Then plant your small plants in the container. Leave space between the plants so they can grow. Water the plants lightly. Then put a lid on the top of the container. Set the container in a warm place where it will get some light. If the inside of the container gets too wet, open the lid for a while.

Is the information clear and easy to follow?

Yes, the information is clear and easy to follow.

What information might the student have included?

The student might have said how large the glass container should be or what plants would work well in the container.

Test Yourself

Read the writing prompt below. Then plan, write, and proofread your response.

> Write a paragraph explaining how you play your favorite game.

Use the space below to plan what you are going to write. Then write your response on a separate sheet of paper.

Standards 3.5.4, 3.5.7

In Unit 3, you read samples of literary texts. These included stories, poems, and plays. Some of the things you had to pay attention to were the same as when you read for information. You look for the main idea. You give reasons why things happen. You connect what you're reading to what you know.

In literary texts there are other things to notice, too. The setting and characters are important. You need to note details about what characters are like and why they act certain ways. You need to understand the problems they face and how they solve them.

It's the same when you're *writing* about stories, poems, or plays. Think about how writing a book report is different from writing a social studies report. Think about how writing about a poem is different from writing about a real person's life.

On a test, you may be asked to answer questions about literary texts with a short response or an extended response. A short response can be a few words up to a paragraph. An extended response is an essay, which is a few paragraphs long. For extended responses, it's important to follow the steps of the writing process.

On a test, think about these things:

- **Who the characters are and what they are like.** Think about how they relate to one another and why they do the things they do.

- **The setting of the story.** Where and when does it take place? How does the setting help create the feeling of the story?

- **The structure of the story.** Pay attention to the order of events. Note what happens in the beginning, middle, and end.

- **The problems in the story.** What are the problems? Which characters are affected? How are the problems solved?

- **The theme of the story.** What lesson does it teach?
- **Which graphic organizer might help organize details.**
  For example, a web can help you understand a character.
  A sequence chart can help you see the order of events.

Guided Practice

Read this poem. Then answer the questions.

The Day the Gerbils Got Out

by Judith Lipsett

There's a day I'll always remember.
Of this I have no doubt.
It was November twenty-fifth—
The day the gerbils got out.

5 They usually live at my school,
But we had a four-day break.
I said I'd take the gerbils home,
And that was my first mistake.

Their names are Midge and Morty.
10 Their cage is sturdy and strong,
But only when the door is latched
Will they stay where they belong.

My cousins were with us for dinner,
For it was of course Turkey Day.
15 Sonia, Sally, Steven, and Sam,
And the littlest, Annie May.

Well, Annie is full of mischief,
As I found out that night.
While we ate our candied yams
20 She tiptoed out of sight.

She opened up the little latch
And then sat on the floor
As those two gerbils figured out
That they could now explore.

25 She watched as they ran by her,
   Away like birds they flew.
   What they would do from then on,
   She didn't have a clue.

   We all were full after dinner,
30 Couldn't eat another bite.
   Well, maybe some pumpkin pie—
   Yes, that would be all right.

   My mom went into the kitchen
   To make some sweet whip cream.
35 But when she put it on a pie,
   My mom began to scream!

   We all ran in to help her
   And saw, to our surprise,
   There were those two gerbils,
40 Up to their whiskers in pies!

Read these lines from the poem.

> *Well, Annie is full of mischief,*
> *As I found out that night.*

What do these lines tell you about Annie?

_____

_____

_____

_____

_____

You know from the poem that letting the gerbils escape was not really an accident. Annie knew what she was doing. Here is a sample answer:

These lines tell that Annie is a troublemaker, and that she will show this later in the poem. You find out that Annie opened the latch on the gerbil cage.

Explain how you could predict what was going to happen in the poem. Use examples from the poem in your answer.

In your answer, be sure to explain:

- what information the author gives you before you know what the poem will be about

- what event or details help you predict what happens

- what probably happens after the end of the poem

Read the question again carefully. It's a question about predicting events. You're being asked to describe details that help you predict what will happen in the poem, and what might happen in the story after the poem ends. So the first step of prewriting should be organizing the important details. Here's a sample answer. Notice how the essay is organized into paragraphs that answer each of the points in the question.

The title of the poem tells what is going to happen in the poem. You know that the gerbils are going to get out before you even read the first lines of the poem.

Lines 11–12 tell you that the gerbils will run out of their cage if the door is open. This is a good clue about how the gerbils will escape. They will run out of their cage through an open door. Lines 17–24 tell you about little cousin Annie, and how she opens the latch on the gerbils' cage. Annie is "full of mischief." She wants the gerbils to escape. It is a special holiday with a lot of people over for dinner. This helps to predict that something funny will happen next.

The final detail that helps predict what happens is "My mom began to scream!" This is a good clue that she sees the gerbils. When everyone runs into the kitchen, they see the gerbils in the pies.

When the poem ends, you can predict that the family will catch the gerbils and put them back in their cage.

Test Yourself

Read the story. Then answer the question.

You Can't Please Everyone

a folktale from Great Britain

Once, a man, his son, and their donkey went to market to sell grain. On the way home, they met a farmer. "Fools," the farmer berated them. "You have a donkey that is carrying nothing, and yet you walk beside him. One of you should ride."

Following the farmer's advice, the man lifted his son onto the donkey. By and by, they came to a spring where two women were filling pails with water. "What a terrible thing," one of the women said. "Young people have no manners. The healthy boy rides like a king. His hardworking father walks."

So the man told his son to get off the donkey, and he got on instead. Soon, they came to a tree. Two men were sitting in the shade. When they saw the travelers, one of the men said, "What a cruel thing. Here is a big, strong man riding a donkey. Yet he makes his son walk. He should treat his child better."

Therefore, the man lifted his son onto the donkey's back so both could ride. By and by, they came to their town. A group of townspeople began to point and speak about them. "Such a thoughtless man and his selfish son," they said. "They make their poor animal work so hard. How would they like it if they had to carry the donkey?"

So the man and boy found a sturdy pole and tied the donkey's feet to it. Then they lifted the pole and carried the donkey. They did not understand why everyone they passed from that point on was laughing.

Finally, they arrived home, tired and sore. When the man told his wife all that had happened, she said, "That should teach you a lesson. Everyone has an opinion, but you don't have to do what everyone tells you."

1 What kind of person is the man in this story? Use details from the story to support your answer.

Be sure to include:

- a title for your essay

- a clear beginning, middle, and end

- specific details from the story to describe the man and support your ideas

Use the space below to plan what you are going to write. Write a title for your essay. Then write your response on a separate sheet of paper.

Test-Taking Tips

You have just prepared yourself to take reading tests. You have practiced 12 important reading skills. You can identify questions for each of these skills on a test. The only thing left to do now is to take a test. Here are some ways to be at your best on test days.

- **Go to bed early the night before a test.** You want to be rested and wide awake.

- **Eat a good breakfast.** This will help keep your brain and body working at their best.

- **Be prepared.** Bring two pencils with you.

- **Follow all directions.** If something is not clear, ask your teacher to explain.

- **Make sure the item number on your answer sheet matches the number of the question.**

- **Answer all the questions.** If you are not sure, choose the answer that makes the most sense.

- **Look over all the answer choices.** First, look for answers that you know are wrong. Then think about the other answers and decide which one is right.

- **Check the clock.** Tests are timed, so do not spend too much time on any one question. Skip it and come back to it later if you do not know the answer.

- **Keep up with your schoolwork all year long.** That is how you learn the skills you need for taking tests.

Part 1

Read this story about how a girl and her grandfather solved a problem. Then answer the questions.

 ## A Penny Saved

Serena and Grandpa walked down Front Street. Serena stopped to look at the red and white soccer shoes in the window of Miller's Sporting Goods Store. If only she could have them! Maybe she could ask her mother to buy them for her birthday. No, her birthday was six months away. Could she ask her father to buy them when they went back-to-school shopping? No, school had just ended for the summer. She might be able to borrow her sister's babysitting money. No, Tara needed that money herself.

"Why so sad, Serena?" Grandpa asked.

"Oh, it's no big deal," Serena said, but she sounded unhappy.

"Is it those shoes?" her grandpa asked. "I could buy them for you, but I have a better idea. Remember the big jar of pennies I gave you on your birthday?"

Serena did remember. Grandpa had given Serena a jar of pennies and suggested she start a coin collection. Serena planned to, but she never got around to it. She knew there were four or five hundred pennies in the jar. But that was only four or five dollars, not nearly enough to buy the shoes.

"Let's look at those pennies carefully," Grandpa said.

Back home, Serena spilled the pennies into a pile on the kitchen table. Grandpa helped her sort them. Each penny had the year it was made stamped into the metal. A few were very old. Some were from the 1920s! Grandpa selected just four of the pennies.

He said, "This one is worth about two dollars. These two are worth about five dollars each. And this one is very rare. A man at the coin shop told me it's worth at least $20!"

Serena's eyes lit up like bright lights. "That's enough to buy the shoes," she cheered.

"It certainly is," her grandpa agreed. "When I gave you those pennies, I was hoping you would get interested in collecting coins. I picked the pennies carefully. Some are worth just one cent. Others are worth a nickel or a dime. The very special ones, like these four, are worth quite a bit."

Serena kissed her grandpa. Now she had enough money for the shoes she wanted, and she had a new hobby.

1   What is the MAIN problem in this story?

   A   Serena needs money to buy a birthday gift.

   B   Grandpa wants to get rid of his old coin collection.

   C   Serena wants money to buy something she sees at a store.

   D   Grandpa is worried about Serena because she seems so sad.

2   During which month of the year does this story PROBABLY take place?

   A   December

   B   February

   C   March

   D   June

3 Read these lines from the story.

"These two are worth about five dollars each. And this one is very rare."

What does the word *rare* mean?

A big

B new

C shiny

D unusual

4 Which word BEST describes Serena's grandfather?

A silly

B kind

C quiet

D sneaky

5 In the future, Serena will PROBABLY become very interested in

A playing soccer

B going shopping

C collecting coins

D babysitting children

6 Why had Serena's grandfather given her a jar of pennies?

A He was cleaning out his house.

B He knew she liked to collect coins.

C He was giving away all of his things.

D He hoped she would start a collection.

7 How is the problem in the passage solved?

    A Serena uses some valuable pennies.

    B Tara gives Serena her babysitting money.

    C Serena gets what she wants for her birthday.

    D Serena's mom and dad solve the problem for her.

8 The story is being told from the point of view of

    A Serena

    B a narrator

    C Grandfather

    D Tara

9 Which word from the passage is NOT a compound word?

    A downtown

    B vacation

    C birthday

    D grandfather

Read this story about a famous president. Then answer the questions.

Abraham Lincoln

by Curtis Wright

Who was the greatest president of the United States? Some will say George Washington. He has been called "the father of our country." Others will tell you that Thomas Jefferson was number one. He wrote the Declaration of Independence. Still, some will insist that the greatest president was Abraham Lincoln.

Lincoln went from being a poor boy to being a wealthy man. He led the country through the most difficult time in our history. A law that he signed helped put an end to slavery in the country. You can see a picture of Abraham Lincoln on U.S. pennies and on the five-dollar bill.

As a boy and a young man, Lincoln went by the nickname Abe. Some people called him "honest Abe" because he was known to keep his word. Abe was born in Kentucky. Then his family moved to Indiana. He grew up in a small log cabin in the woods. Abe loved to read. Since there was no electricity in those days, he read by the light of the fireplace. He did not go to school very much. In those days, few children on the frontier were able to get much schooling. But Abe learned so much from the books he read.

Abe worked at many different jobs. He cut wood with an ax. He did farm work. Later he worked in a store. After a while, he became a lawyer. Then he ran for office. Sometimes he lost. But he kept trying. In 1861, Abe became president of the United States.

The First 16 U.S. Presidents

1	George Washington	9	William Henry Harrison
2	John Adams	10	John Tyler
3	Thomas Jefferson	11	James Polk
4	James Madison	12	Zachary Taylor
5	James Monroe	13	Millard Fillmore
6	John Quincy Adams	14	Franklin Pierce
7	Andrew Jackson	15	James Buchanan
8	Martin Van Buren	16	Abraham Lincoln

The job was not easy for the new leader. People in the country were not getting along. Rich farmers in the South used slaves to do their field work. Many people in the North thought slavery was evil and must end. There were other problems as well.

Lincoln wanted peace, but there was no peace. The country went to war. The Civil War was one of the worst times in the country's history. In some cases, brother actually fought against brother. It was a horrible war, but it ended when the North won. Then the nation needed to be <u>rebuilt</u>.

Abe Lincoln would have helped the country heal its wounds. But that was not to be. Many people from the South were still angry with him. A man named John Wilkes Booth killed Lincoln. When he died, people from all over the country came together to remember him. Today, most people think he was one of the very best men in our country's history.

10 What is the meaning of the word *rebuilt* in paragraph 6?

A fixed

B moved

C changed

D destroyed

11 According to the table, which number president was Abraham Lincoln?

A tenth

B twelfth

C fifteenth

D sixteenth

12 This passage is BEST described as

A poetry

B a fable

C an essay

D nonfiction

13 The author MOST LIKELY wrote this passage to

A entertain readers

B explain how to do something

C describe Abraham Lincoln's life

D persuade readers

14 In which way is this passage MOST like the story "A Penny Saved" from the beginning of this practice test?

A Both are about things from long, long ago.

B Both show the man whose face is on pennies.

C Both are about a problem with a happy ending.

D Both tell about a horrible war.

15 Which happened FIRST in this passage?

A Abe Lincoln worked hard and learned a lot by reading.

B Abe Lincoln cut wood with an ax, worked on a farm, and worked in a store.

C The U.S. had a big problem because people from the North fought against people from the South.

D Abe Lincoln was elected president during a tough time for the country.

Read the passage. Then answer the questions.

What Is a Vole?

by Charlotte McCormick

A vole is one of the smallest kinds of mammals. People are mammals. So are dogs, and cats, and elephants. Mice and rats are also mammals. A vole looks a lot like a small mouse or rat, but there are some clear differences. There are actually about 70 different kinds of voles. Each kind is unique in some way. But they are all different from mice and rats in some important ways.

For one thing, voles usually do not come into homes or buildings. They live outdoors. They dig holes called burrows. Most voles eat only plants. But they can still be pests when they eat plants from people's gardens.

Also, voles are very small. Most mammals are larger. Even mice and rats are bigger than most voles. Voles have thick bodies with short legs. They also have short tails and small eyes. Their tiny ears are partly hidden. Their fur is stiff. It can be dark brown or gray.

The most interesting thing about voles is how they live in families. For a while, male and female voles show no interest in each other. Then, all of a sudden, a female vole smells something about a certain male vole. He becomes her mate, and she will have no other. They stay together as long as they live.

Scientists think the smell from the male causes a change in the female's brain. From then on, all she wants to do is start a family with that male. One scientist said, "It's kind of like falling in love and never falling out." The mother and father vole have babies. They are good parents and take good care of their children.

Sometimes people fall in love and stay together for the rest of their lives. Some scientists wonder if there is something in some people's brains that makes them just a little bit like voles.

16 Read the sentence from the passage.

They dig holes called burrows.

What is the predicate, or verb, in this sentence?

A They

B dig

C holes

D burrows

17 Which sentence from the passage is an OPINION?

A Voles usually do not come into homes or buildings.

B A vole is one of the smallest kinds of mammals.

C There are actually about 70 different kinds of voles.

D The most interesting thing about voles is how they live in families.

18 Paragraph 4 is MAINLY about how voles

A dig holes

B eat plants

C start families

D look like mice

19 Read the sentence from the passage.

Each kind is unique in some way.

What does the word *unique* mean?

A large and heavy

B strong and healthy

C special or different

D nasty and troublesome

Carla is writing a report about the beginnings of the game of basketball. Use the pages from books she is using to gather information to answer the questions in numbers 20 and 21.

20 What is this page of a book called?

F

field goal A made basket that scores two points (see also three-point field goal)

flagrant foul A foul in which a player uses far too much force in a situation that is against the rules

foul A foul is a play or situation that is against the rules. Most fouls involve making contact with another player. Some other fouls include breaking rules for the number of players on the floor, dribbling incorrectly, and shooting after the 24-second clock counts down to zero.

A the cover

B the glossary

C the title page

D the table of contents

21 What is this page of a book called?

A the index

B the glossary

C the title page

D the table of contents

Read this passage about a rain shower. Then answer the questions.

Nature's Wash Day

Author Unknown

Mother Nature had a wash day
   And called upon the showers
To bathe the dusty faces
   Of the little roadside flowers.
5 She scrubbed the green grass carpet
   Until it shone like <u>new</u>.
She washed the faded dresses
   Of the oaks and maples, too.
No shady nook or corner
10   Escaped her searching <u>eye</u>,
And then she sent the friendly sun
   To shine and make them dry.

22 Which word in the passage rhymes with the word *eye?*

    A day

    B green

    C oaks

    D dry

23 Read these lines from the poem again.

> *Mother Nature had a wash day*
>   *And called upon the <u>showers</u>*
> *To bathe the dusty faces*
>   *Of the little roadside flowers.*

Which word means the same as the word *showers?*

    A rains

    B backs

    C parties

    D people

24 Which thing in the poem is called "friendly"?

    A the sun

    B the grass

    C the dresses

    D the flowers

25 Read these lines from the poem.

And then she sent the friendly sun
To shine and make them <u>dry</u>.

Which word means the opposite of the word *dry?*

A wet

B cold

C crumbly

D clean

26 Read these lines from the poem.

She washed the faded dresses
Of the oaks and maples, too.

These lines tell about how the rain cleans the

A air

B trees

C streets

D ground

Kevin wrote a letter to a relative who lives far away. Read the letter. Then answer the questions.

> 309 East Valley Street
> Fort Wayne IN 46801
> July 1, 2009
>
> Dear Uncle Ron,
>
> **1** How are things in Alaska **2** Thank you for mailing me the book of pictures. **3** They are just beautiful! **4** Someday I hope to visit you. **5** My neighbor has been to Mexico. **6** Here in Fort Wayne, we are getting ready for the fourth of july. **7** There will be a parade on Saturday. **8** At night there will be fireworks in the park. **9** Please say hello to both of my cousins and to Aunt Rose for me. **10** I will write you again soon. **11** I will also call you on your birthday.
>
> Love,
> Kevin

27 What is the correct way to write the second line of Kevin's address?

   A Fort, Wayne IN 46801

   B Fort Wayne, IN 46801

   C Fort Wayne IN, 46801

   D Correct as it is

28 Which sentence does NOT belong in the letter?

   A Thank you for mailing me the book of pictures.

   B They are just beautiful!

   C Someday I hope to visit you.

   D My neighbor has been to Mexico.

29 Which is the correct way to write Sentence 6?

   A Here in fort wayne, we are getting ready for the fourth of july.

   B Here in Fort Wayne, we are getting ready for the Fourth of july.

   C Here in Fort Wayne, we are getting ready for the Fourth of July.

   D Correct as it is

Part 2

Read the passage. Then answer the questions that follow.

It was unusual for Roman to be <u>this</u> <u>late</u>. He was supposed to <u>meet</u> Clare in front of the <u>school</u> at four. Clare called Roman's <u>home</u> many times, but no one answered. Then she checked the library and the cafeteria. It seemed like Roman had disappeared. One <u>hour</u> later, when Clare was about to go home, Roman finally arrived.

"I'm not late," explained Roman. "We were supposed to meet at five. You must have misunderstood."

Clare was a little angry, but mostly she was happy that Roman was safe.

Choose an underlined word from the story that has the same vowel sound. Write it on the line.

30 power   _____

31 know   _____

32 paint   _____

33 clean   _____

34 rule   _____

35 inch   _____

Read this story written by a boy named Malcolm. Then answer the questions that follow.

It's the end of the year and I didn't want to go to school today. Our class was supposed to go to Lake Michigan. I had been there before and didn't want to go again, especially to see some old boat. I'd rather stay home to play computer games and go skateboarding. But my mom made me go anyway.

So I went to school and to the fishing harbor. That's where the boat is. When we got on board, we met Captain Dooley, the "Admiral of the Lake." That's the name people gave him because he knows Lake Michigan so well. Captain Dooley takes school kids out on the lake. He teaches them about its history, the plant and animal life, and how to help save it from pollution. I thought this was going to be boring.

Then Captain Dooley started telling us stories about his life. He was born in 1925 and grew up near Chicago. His dad taught him and his brothers to catch fish. Captain Dooley talked about the first time his dad took him out on the lake to fish for salmon. He was only 14. The weather was so cold that his hands almost froze.

Five years later Captain Dooley began working full time on Lake Michigan. He worked there for more than 50 years on fishing boats. Now he works on the lake to teach kids all the interesting things about it.

Before I knew it, the boat was back at the harbor. I was disappointed because there wasn't time for Captain Dooley's story about a big storm in the 1950s. Maybe I can get my mom to take me there again. I'm kind of glad she made me go today, after all.

36 How does Malcolm feel at the end of the story?
Use details from the story to support your answer.

_____

_____

_____

_____

_____

_____

37 Captain Dooley may no longer be working as a fisherman,
but he is still dedicated to Lake Michigan. Give examples
from the story that support this statement.

_____

_____

_____

_____

_____

_____

Read this story and answer the question that follows.

Jada loves desserts. She loves chocolate cake and strawberry pie. She loves cherry tarts, honey buns, and lemon cookies. But she really loves ice cream the most, especially ice cream sundaes.

"I'm sure of it!" exclaimed Jada. "This is the best sundae I have ever created. It's exactly the way I like it. It's perfect!"

Jada sank her spoon into a mountain of ice cream—three heaping scoops of the creamiest vanilla you can buy. It was the kind with tiny specks of ground vanilla beans. She topped this with a river of hot fudge. It was just hot enough to begin melting the ice cream. On top of this, she added mounds of whipped cream. She sprinkled some chopped walnuts over the whipped cream. Then she added a big red juicy cherry on the very top.

"Mmm," sighed Jada. "This tastes fantastic. There is nothing like a hot fudge sundae. It's hot, cold, soft, smooth, crunchy, and sweet!"

38 Why is this sundae the best one Jada has ever created? Use details from the story to support your answer.

_____

_____

_____

_____

_____

_____

Now read this story about rain forests and answer the questions that follow.

The world's rain forests are amazing places! Many different kinds of animals live there. Colorful birds and giant snakes live in rain forests. Poison frogs, fruit bats, and jaguars live there, too. Sadly, these forests are quickly being destroyed. People cut down trees to get lumber for homes. This ruins many animals' homes. They are left with nowhere to go. Here are some more facts about rain forests:

- Rain forests are home to over half of the world's species. That is millions of plants and animals!

- Rain forest plants and trees make at least one-third of Earth's oxygen. Some people even call the forests the "lungs of the world."

- Rain falls almost every day in the rain forests. They can get over 80 inches of rain per year!

- One hundred acres of forest are destroyed each minute. Some experts think that the forests will be gone in 40 years.

- Rain forest plants are used in many new kinds of drugs to help fight disease and illness.

- Many foods you eat came from rain forests. They include oranges, sugar, vanilla, cocoa, lemons, peanuts, and more!

- Rain forests have been around for 70 to 100 million years. Even dinosaurs roamed the world's rain forests.

39 What would happen if the rain forests were destroyed? Explain two effects.

1)_____

_____

_____

2)_____

_____

_____

40 What do you think is the author's MAIN purpose for writing this article? Use details to support your answer.

_____

_____

_____

_____

_____

_____

Read the selection and answer the question.

Dragons

What comes to your mind when you think of a dragon? Do you picture a huge creature with scaly skin like a reptile? Does it have strong legs, claws like a lion, and wings like a bat? Does it breathe fire? Then you have probably read stories that end like this: "The brave knight showed up on his white horse just in time to save the young maiden from certain death. He killed the fierce dragon with his sword." Of course, dragons aren't real. They are just mythical (make-believe) creatures that you read about in fairy tales or see in scary movies. Right?

Komodo dragon

Wrong! Dragons do exist in the real world—Komodo dragons. They don't have wings or breathe fire like mythical dragons. But they are just as fierce and dangerous. They even attack and kill people. Other animals run and hide when they see this dragon coming. A Komodo dragon can smell its prey from five miles away. It eats anything, dead or alive. It will fight off whatever gets in its way.

The Komodo dragon has scaly skin and a yellow snakelike tongue. It uses its tongue to pick up the scent of other animals. Its rows of sharp teeth look like a saw. It has a long neck and tail and powerful legs with claws. It can grow up to 10 feet in length and reach a weight of 300 pounds.

Komodo dragons live on a few islands in the Pacific Ocean. They get their name from one of the islands.

41 Compare and contrast what the selection says about the mythical dragon and the real Komodo dragon. Fill in the Venn diagram from the selection.

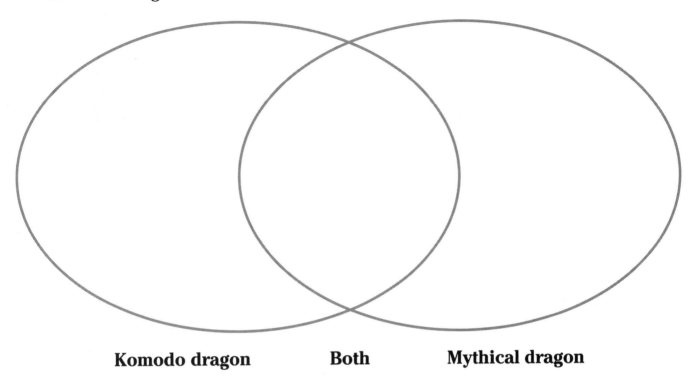

Komodo dragon   **Both**   **Mythical dragon**

Read the selection. Then answer the questions that follow.

Brave Casey Jones

A train engineer is a person who drives a train. Casey Jones is one of the most famous train engineers. He drove a train called the *Cannonball Express.* Casey and his train were known for always being on time. He knew people depended on him.

On April 29, 1900, Casey drove the *Cannonball Express* into Memphis right on time. As he was about to go home, he learned that the next driver was sick. Who would drive the train? How would the passengers get where they needed to go? Casey knew what he had to do.

Casey offered to drive the train. The train left the station after midnight. It was 95 minutes late leaving. Casey didn't want the passengers to be late. He was determined to make up the time. With the help of fireman Sim Webb, he went as fast as he could.

At around 4:00 A.M., Casey approached Vaughan, Mississippi. He was only two minutes behind schedule. Then Casey saw another train stopped on the track ahead of him. Casey knew he couldn't stop his train in time. It was going to hit the other train.

Casey could have jumped off the train, but he didn't. He told Sim Webb to jump off the train instead. Then he stayed on the train and used the brake to slow it down. Casey Jones died when the *Cannonball Express* hit the other train. Sim Webb and all the passengers lived. Casey's bravery had saved everyone on the train.

The story of Casey Jones was made famous in a song. The song celebrates Casey's courage. People still sing "The Ballad of Casey Jones" today.

42 What genre is this passage?

_____

_____

_____

_____

43 How can you tell?

_____

_____

_____

_____

Read the poem "Four Seasons." Then answer the questions that follow.

Four Seasons

by Anne Sophie Bachelder

Orange leaves whisper in chilly, crisp air.
A smiling jack-o-lantern sits on a chair.
Thanksgiving is near; the nights seem to crawl,
My feeling is that it must be fall.

5 Butterflies flutter and float on the breeze,
Pink flowers are budding on all of the trees.
Baby birds in their nests twitter and sing,
My feeling is that it must be spring.

The sun rules the sky like a golden king,
10 It beams with big hopes of the fun it will bring.
For only three months—that's a real bummer.
My feeling is that it must be summer.

Snowflakes fall gently and float to the ground.
They fall without talking, not ever a sound,
15 Sparkling like sugar and magical glitter.
My feeling is that it must be winter.

44 Which line from the poem has a word that sounds like
what it means?

_____

_____

_____

_____

45 Find two examples of an object in the poem that is described as doing something human. What is it, and what did it do that is like a person? Use details from the poem in your answer.

1)_____

_____

_____

2)_____

_____

_____

Part 3

Read the writing prompt below. Then plan, write, and proofread your response.

> Think about a restaurant you have visited. Write about this restaurant. Use details to describe this place and bring it to life.

Here are some questions to help you think about what you will write.

- What does the restaurant look like?
- What did you eat at the restaurant?
- What was the service like?
- Was the restaurant crowded?

Use the space below to plan what you are going to write. Write your response on a separate sheet of paper.